Donald O. Clifton
1924-2003

Inventor of the Clifton StrengthsFinder® and recognized as
the Father of Strengths-Based Psychology by an American
Psychological Association Presidential Commendation

STRENGTHS

BASED

LEADERSHIP

GREAT LEADERS, TEAMS, AND WHY PEOPLE FOLLOW

FROM GALLUP

TOM RATH

GALLUP PRESS
1330 Avenue of the Americas
17th Floor
New York, NY 10019

Library of Congress Control Number: 2008937114
ISBN: 978-1-59562-025-5

First Printing: 2008
22

Printed in Canada

♻ This book was printed on chlorine-free paper made with
   100% post-consumer waste.

To the pioneering researcher, Don Clifton
(1924-2003), who spent four decades studying the strengths
of great leaders

TABLE OF CONTENTS

A NOTE OF THANKS TO OUR TEAM

Gallup has been studying human behavior for more than 70 years and consulting with organizational leaders for more than four decades. Over the years, hundreds of top scientists and leadership consultants have contributed to this collective knowledge base. Even as we write this book, Gallup consultants around the globe are spending their days working with leaders to improve their organizations' effectiveness. It is the work of the following team of experts, many of whom have devoted their lives to studying great leaders, that fills the pages of this book.

Vandana Allman	Curt Liesveld
Jim Asplund	Mary Pat Loos
Dana Baugh	Rachel Maglinger
Cheryl Beamer	Jacque Merritt
Brian Brim	Jan Miller
Jim Clifton	Jane Miller
Tonya Fredstrom	Laura Mussman
Andrew Green	Peter Ong
Christy Hammer	Connie Rath
Anne Harbison	Tony Rutigliano
Jim Harter	Rosemary Travis
Tim Hodges	Paula Walker
Rodd Karr	Stosh Walsh
Lalit Khanna	Damian Welch

In addition to this team of leadership experts, there were many who shaped the content of this book and its accompanying website. Our publishing team, led by business book gurus Larry Emond and Piotrek Juszkiewicz, pushed us at every turn to tell a better story. Then our world-class editors, Geoff Brewer and Kelly Henry, refined this manuscript countless times and taught us how to be more effective writers along the way. The following members of our core team spent countless hours working on the research, content, and technology that went into *Strengths Based Leadership*: Samantha Allemang, Sangeeta Badal, Jason Carr, Swati Jain, Trista Kunce, Emily Meyer, and Joy Murphy.

Beyond this core team, we would also like to thank all the people who reviewed drafts of this book, the team who created the website, our research group, and in particular, the many critical friends in our client partnerships who kept us true to our mission and science and provided many of the subjects of our studies. Without these great partners, this book would not have been possible. And to all of the leaders who gave us their time, we extend our most sincere thanks and gratitude.

INTRODUCTION

The best leaders get to live on.

Think for a moment about the leaders you respect — whether they lead countries, organizations, communities, or families — who continue to live on because of the way they have shaped your thoughts and beliefs. Even though you may not notice it in the moment, the most effective leaders forever alter the course of your life.

Chances are, you will have many opportunities to lead during your own lifetime. If you're able to seize these opportunities, your influence will continue to grow for generations to come. Maybe it's the desire to make a lasting impact on the world that drives so many of us to want to lead.

In a recent Gallup Poll, we asked people to rate their own leadership ability. Out of 1,001 people randomly surveyed, 97% rated their ability to lead as being at or above average. And more than two-thirds said they have led a group or team. The fact is, whether you are taking charge in a boardroom, on a construction site, or even in your home, it is likely that you will find yourself leading at some point in your life.

So what are the keys to being a more effective leader? To answer this question, we assembled a team of experts to review decades of Gallup data on this topic, which included more than 20,000 in-depth interviews with senior leaders, studies of more than one million work teams, and 50 years of Gallup Polls about the world's most admired leaders. Our team then initiated a study of more than 10,000 *followers* around the world. In this study, we asked followers to tell us — in their own words — why they follow the most influential leader in their life.

Three key findings emerged from this research:

1. *The most effective leaders are always investing in strengths.*

   In the workplace, when an organization's leadership fails to focus on individuals' strengths, the odds of an employee being engaged are a dismal 1 in 11 (9%). But when an organization's leadership focuses on the strengths of its employees, the odds soar to almost 3 in 4 (73%). So that means when leaders focus on and invest in their employees' strengths, the odds of each person being engaged goes up *eightfold*. As we will review in Part One, this increase in engagement translates into substantial gains for the organization's bottom line *and* each employee's well-being.

2. *The most effective leaders surround themselves with the right people and then maximize their team.*

   While the best leaders are not well-rounded, the best teams are. Our research found that top-performing teams have strengths in four specific domains. In Part

Two, you will hear from four well-known leaders as they describe how their strengths play out in these domains. You will also see how one CEO maximized his existing team and learn about the elements that differentiated the top-performing teams we studied from the rest of the pack.

3. *The most effective leaders understand their followers' needs.*

People follow leaders for very specific reasons. When we asked thousands of followers, they were able to describe exactly what they need from a leader with remarkable clarity. In Part Three, we will review the results from this study and tell you more about followers' four basic needs.

To help you learn about your own strengths as a leader, you will have the opportunity to take a new leadership version of Gallup's StrengthsFinder program. (See "Taking StrengthsFinder" in the Additional Resources section of this book.) Following an online assessment, you will receive a guide that shows you how your top five strengths fit into the four domains of leadership strength (from Part Two). The guide will also give you specific suggestions for meeting the basic needs of those who look to you for leadership (from Part Three). But as you will learn from some of the most effective leaders we've studied, the path to great leadership starts with a deep understanding of the strengths you bring to the table.

PART ONE:

INVESTING IN YOUR STRENGTHS

If you spend your life trying to be good at everything, you will never be great at anything. While our society encourages us to be well-rounded, this approach inadvertently breeds mediocrity. Perhaps the greatest misconception of all is that of the well-rounded leader.

Organizations are quick to look for leaders who are great communicators, visionary thinkers, and who can also get things done and follow through. All of these attributes are desirable and necessary for an organization to succeed. But of all the leaders we have studied, we have yet to find one who has world-class strength in *all* of these areas. Sure, many leaders can get by or are above average in several domains. But paradoxically, those who strive to be competent in all areas become the least effective leaders overall.

LEADING BY IMITATION

Sarah has a knot in her stomach as she drives to work on Monday morning. While she rarely looks forward to the start of a workweek, today the mere thought of going to the office is making her ill. While driving through traffic, Sarah begins to wonder why this particular Monday is so much worse. She's perplexed because last Friday was one of the best days in the office she could remember.

As Sarah pulls into the parking lot, she figures out why the end of last week was so enjoyable: Her boss, Bob, was out of town. That was the good news. The bad news is that he was attending *yet another* course that would equip him to be a better leader. As Sarah walks across the parking lot, her stomach tightens even more when she remembers what happened the last time Bob went to one of those leadership retreats.

Earlier in the year, Bob had attended a conference that explored Lincoln's leadership style during the Civil War. When he returned, Bob predictably spent the next month trying to teach everyone on his team to be "exceptional communicators." Sarah chuckled at the memory, recalling how awkward this was for the computer programmers in her office, who usually prefer typing to talking. Fortunately, like all Bob's phases, this one came to an abrupt halt once he read a book suggesting that the best leaders had humble personalities, and he subsequently quit pressuring Sarah's more introverted colleagues to be the next Lincoln or Kennedy.

When Sarah enters the building, she has no choice but to pass Bob's office, and the knot in her stomach tightens. As if on cue, Bob waves her in. Reluctantly, Sarah leans against the frame of the open door. In her mind, Sarah is cynically wondering what flavor will be served up this month. But to be cordial, Sarah asks Bob about the retreat.

After telling Sarah how peaceful and serene it was in the small mountain town where the event was held, Bob cuts to the chase. He declares, "My big takeaway from last week was that we all need to be more *adaptive to change* in order to grow our business." Then Bob leans forward, looking at Sarah earnestly, and continues, "We went through this activity where each of us had to map out how quickly we adapt to new market trends. Well, like everyone else, it turns out that we spend nowhere near enough time readying ourselves for big change. If we're going to lead our industry, we need to not only *anticipate*, but better yet, *create* change." Bob rambles on for 10 more minutes, but Sarah had gotten the message right away: The leadership buzzword for the next few weeks or months is going to be "change."

As Sarah walks away from Bob's office, she is already anticipating the moans and groans of her peers when they hear about the latest fad. Then she suddenly realizes something about Bob that almost has her feeling sorry for him. While he has spent much of his career in a leadership role, the vast majority of her boss' efforts have been focused on trying to mimic traits of leaders he has known or read about.

The bookshelf in his office is lined with weighty tomes about famous political and business leaders, dead and alive. When Bob speaks to groups, he frequently quotes the company's CEO and other leaders who have appeared in the media. On occasion, usually when talking to groups of managers and leaders in the organization, Bob even puts together a "greatest hits" list of all the things that he has learned from studying historical leaders and modern-day corporate chiefs. He describes how all leaders must be empathetic, creative, disciplined, strategic, humble, decisive, and of course, great communicators.

Sarah can see that Bob has spent most of his career striving to be just like the leaders he admires. Yet he fails to realize that the people he looks up to are all very different. There is no single person who embodies even half of the characteristics on Bob's exhaustive list of what makes a well-rounded leader. And perhaps most strikingly, the one leader that Bob knows the least about is *himself*.

FINDING YOUR LEADERSHIP STRENGTHS

"I've never met an effective leader who wasn't aware of his talents and working to sharpen them."

— Former NATO Supreme Allied Commander Wesley Clark,
in *The New York Times Magazine*

Without an awareness of your strengths, it's almost impossible for you to lead effectively. We all lead in very different ways, based on our talents and our limitations. Serious problems occur when we think we need to be exactly like the leaders we admire. Doing so takes us out of our natural element and practically eliminates our chances of success.

If you look at great historical leaders such as Winston Churchill or Mahatma Gandhi, you might notice more differences than similarities — and it is the differences that defined them and led to their success. Churchill's bold and commanding leadership succeeded in mobilizing a war-ravaged nation. It is unlikely he would have had as much success if he had tried to emulate Gandhi's calm and quiet approach. Yet

Gandhi's leadership, during India's struggle for independence, was much more effective because he did not try to emulate the domineering leaders of the past. Both men knew their strengths and used them wisely.

All too often, leaders are blind to the obvious when it comes to something of critical importance to them — their own personality. Many political and business leaders have self-concepts that are miles away from reality. They simply don't know their own strengths and weaknesses.

This is the stuff of parody for late-night talk shows, sitcoms, movies, and stand-up comics. And this problem goes far beyond the boss who thinks he's funny, even though people only laugh at his jokes out of obligation. Most people have encountered a leader who is completely unaware of a glaring weakness. We have spoken with several leaders who claim to be great at developing their people, but when we interview the people they lead, we hear a very different story. In some cases, the leaders in question may be better at demoralizing than developing people. At its worst, this lack of self-awareness can lead to masses of disengaged employees, unhappy customers, and undue stress beyond the workplace.

Although less noticeable, another serious problem occurs when people try to lead while having no clue about their natural strengths. Unfortunately, few people have discovered the place in life where they have the most potential for growth. Based on an analysis of Gallup's 2007 global client database, the vast majority of people *do not* have "the opportunity to do what they do best every day" in their current job. (See chart below.) This problem runs rampant in workplaces throughout the world.

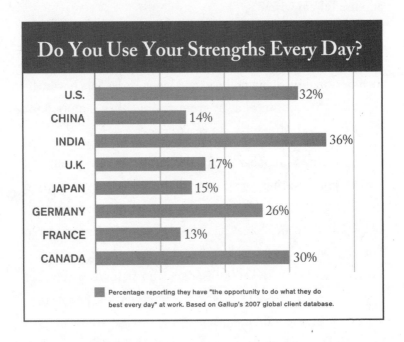

Do You Use Your Strengths Every Day?

U.S.	32%
CHINA	14%
INDIA	36%
U.K.	17%
JAPAN	15%
GERMANY	26%
FRANCE	13%
CANADA	30%

Percentage reporting they have "the opportunity to do what they do best every day" at work. Based on Gallup's 2007 global client database.

It was this problem that led the late leadership researcher and Father of Strengths Psychology, Dr. Donald O. Clifton, to begin studying the unique strengths of leaders. Beginning in the 1960s, Clifton, along with his colleagues from Gallup and the academic world, conducted more than 20,000 interviews with people in leadership roles across almost all industries and occupations, including former heads of state and other global leaders.

Each of these 90-minute interviews was carefully structured; for most of the interviews, the various leaders were asked the exact same questions. This allowed for side-by-side comparisons of leaders' responses. For many business leaders in this study, data on the leader's actual performance were available. This allowed Clifton and his team to compare the best leaders to those who were less successful, based on objective measures.

After all of this research, you might think that a team of scientists would find at least one strength that *all* of the best leaders shared. But when Clifton was asked, just a few months before his death in 2003, what his greatest discovery was from three decades of leadership research, this was his response:

A leader needs to know his strengths as a carpenter knows his tools, or as a physician knows the instruments at her disposal. What great leaders have in common is that each truly knows his or her strengths — and can call on the right strength at the right time. This explains why there is no definitive list of characteristics that describes all leaders.

To help aspiring leaders identify their strengths, Clifton and his team created a web-based program dubbed "StrengthsFinder." As a part of this book, you will have an opportunity to take a new leadership version of the StrengthsFinder program. In addition to helping you discover your own strengths to lead, this new version will provide you with several strategies for leading others based on *their* unique strengths. As you can see in the chart below, if you are able to help the people you lead focus on their strengths, it will dramatically boost engagement levels throughout your organization.

Chances of Being Engaged at Work

ORGANIZATION'S LEADERSHIP DOES NOT FOCUS ON STRENGTHS — 9%

ORGANIZATION'S LEADERSHIP FOCUSES ON STRENGTHS — 73%

A LONG-TERM INVESTMENT

As one top executive summarized, "If you focus on people's weaknesses, they lose confidence." At a very basic level, it is hard for us to build self-confidence when we are focused on our weaknesses instead of our strengths. Over the past decade, Gallup scientists have explored in much more detail the mechanism through which a strengths-based approach influences our lives. These studies revealed that people experience significant gains in self-confidence after taking

StrengthsFinder and learning more about their strengths. This increase in confidence at an individual level may help explain how strengths-based programs boost an organization's overall engagement and productivity.

The awareness of one's strengths and the subsequent increase in self-confidence it produces might have longer term implications as well, according to a landmark 2008 study led by the University of Florida's Tim Judge. Judge and his colleague Charlice Hurst studied the self-evaluations of 7,660 men and women who were between the ages of 14 and 22 when they were first studied in 1979. These 7,660 participants were followed for the next 25 years, and the measures (which included questions about career success, job status, education, and health) were repeated in 2004.

What Judge and Hurst discovered from this 25-year longitudinal study was quite profound. They found that people with higher self-confidence in 1979 ended up with higher income levels and career satisfaction in 2004. But what was even more striking was the fact that people with high self-confidence in 1979 saw their income increase *at an entirely different rate* compared to those with lower levels of self-confidence.

The people who had more confidence in their abilities at a young age (between 14 and 22) started off with slightly higher income levels — making, on average (in 1979), $3,496 more per year than the low-confidence group. As each year went by, this gap continued to widen. When the researchers reviewed follow-up studies from 2004, the group with higher self-confidence was making $12,821 more annually compared to the average annual income for the lower self-confidence group. The people with higher self-confidence in 1979 continued to capitalize on their disproportionate gains as each year passed.

In addition to the income and career benefits, what Judge and Hurst discovered about the link between early self-confidence and physical health may be even more surprising. When asked about the number of health problems they have that interfere with their work, the group with low self-confidence in 1979 reported almost *three times* as many health problems 25 years later in 2004. Almost unbelievably, the group with high self-evaluations in 1979 reported having *fewer* health problems in 2004 than they did 25 years before.

The results of this study suggest that people who are aware of their strengths and build self-confidence at a young age may reap a "cumulative advantage" that continues to grow over a lifetime. A preliminary Gallup analysis (using the same longitudinal panel from Judge and Hurst's study) suggests that people who report having a chance to use their strengths in the workplace gain a similar advantage. Our research team found that people who had the opportunity to use their strengths early on (between the ages of 15-23) had significantly higher job satisfaction and income levels 26 years later.

These outcomes highlight the value of leaders knowing their own strengths and also reveal how important it is for leaders to help others uncover their strengths as early as possible. If an organization's leaders are able to help each person capitalize on this cumulative advantage, it is likely to create more rapid individual *and* organizational growth. These studies also reveal a mechanism through which a truly strengths-based organization may be able to grow at an entirely different rate for decades to come.

PART TWO:

MAXIMIZING YOUR TEAM

Effective leaders surround themselves with the right people and build on each person's strengths. Yet in most cases, leadership teams are a product of circumstance more than design. Among the executive teams we have studied, team members were selected or promoted based primarily on knowledge or competence. So, the best salesperson becomes the chief sales manager, even if he is not a great people manager. The smartest person in IT winds up as the CIO. The top financial expert gets promoted to CFO, and so on.

Rarely are people recruited to an executive team because their strengths are the best complement to those of the existing team members. When is the last time you heard a leader talking about how your team needed to add a person who not only had the technical competence but who could also help build stronger relationships within the group? Or someone who could help influence others on behalf of the entire team? The vast majority of the time, we recruit by job function — and all but ignore individuals' strengths.

What's worse, when leaders do recruit for strength, they all too often pick people who act, think, or behave like themselves, albeit unintentionally in most cases. It's an age-old dilemma. How is a company supposed to grow, adapt, and change if a domineering CEO continues to pick people who agree with him and who have a similar background and personality?

Israeli President Shimon Peres expressed his views on this topic in an interview with Gallup:

What you have to think of is the potential of the person, not his appearance. And if you can discover hidden potentials, that can make a great difference to your organization. You have to distinguish between loyalty and brilliance. Most leaders prefer loyalty over brilliance; they're afraid that they're going to be undercut. My view is different.

Peres went on to describe the importance of getting talented people on his leadership teams and helping them discover more about their unique strengths.

WHAT MAKES A GREAT LEADERSHIP TEAM?

Over the years, Gallup has studied thousands of executive teams. In most cases, our leadership consultants conduct an in-depth interview with a team's formal leader (usually the CEO) and also conduct interviews with each member of the leadership team. This enables us to compare the strengths of each person sitting around the table so that we can start thinking about each one's individual development and succession planning — and perhaps most importantly, how the team looks as a whole.

As we worked with these leadership teams, we began to see that while each member had his or her own unique strengths, the most cohesive and successful teams possessed broader groupings of strengths. So we went back and initiated our most thorough review of this research to date. From this dataset, four distinct domains of leadership strength emerged: Executing, Influencing, Relationship Building, and Strategic Thinking.

While these categories appear to be general, especially when compared to the specific themes within StrengthsFinder (which you can learn more about in the Additional Resources section), it struck us that these broader categories of strengths could be useful for thinking about how leaders can contribute to a team. A more detailed language may work best for individual development, but these broad domains offer a more practical lens for looking at the composition of a team.

The Four Domains of Leadership Strength

EXECUTING
INFLUENCING
RELATIONSHIP BUILDING
STRATEGIC THINKING

We found that it serves a team well to have a representation of strengths in each of these four domains. Instead of one dominant leader who tries to do everything or individuals who all have similar strengths, contributions from all four domains lead to a strong and cohesive team. *Although individuals need not be well-rounded, teams should be.*

This doesn't mean that each person on a team must have strengths exclusively in a single category. In most cases, each team member will possess some strength in multiple domains. A tool like StrengthsFinder can be useful in determining how all team members can maximize their contribution to the group's collective goals. According to our latest research, the 34 StrengthsFinder themes naturally cluster into these four domains of leadership strength based on a statistical factor analysis and a clinical evaluation by Gallup's top scientists. (See the table below for how the 34 themes sort into the four domains of leadership strength.) As you think about how you can contribute to a team and who you need to surround yourself with, this may be a good starting point.

Executing	Influencing	Relationship Building	Strategic Thinking
ACHIEVER	ACTIVATOR	ADAPTABILITY	ANALYTICAL
ARRANGER	COMMAND	CONNECTEDNESS	CONTEXT
BELIEF	COMMUNICATION	DEVELOPER	FUTURISTIC
CONSISTENCY	COMPETITION	EMPATHY	IDEATION
DELIBERATIVE	MAXIMIZER	HARMONY	INPUT
DISCIPLINE	SELF-ASSURANCE	INCLUDER	INTELLECTION
FOCUS	SIGNIFICANCE	INDIVIDUALIZATION	LEARNER
RESPONSIBILITY	WOO	POSITIVITY	STRATEGIC
RESTORATIVE		RELATOR	

Leaders with dominant strength in the **Executing** domain know how to make things happen. When you need someone to implement a solution, these are the people who will work tirelessly to get it done. Leaders with a strength to execute have the ability to "catch" an idea and make it a reality.

For example, one leader may excel at establishing a quality process using themes such as Deliberative or Discipline, while the next leader will use her Achiever theme to work tirelessly toward a goal. Or a leader with strong Arranger may determine the optimal configuration of people needed to complete a task.

Those who lead by **Influencing** help their team reach a much broader audience. People with strength in this domain are always selling the team's ideas inside and outside the organization. When you need someone to take charge, speak up, and make sure your group is heard, look to someone with the strength to influence.

For example, a leader with a lot of Command or Self-Assurance may use few words, but her confidence will continue to project authority and win followers. In contrast, a leader using Communication or Woo might get people involved by helping individuals feel comfortable and connected to the issue at hand.

Those who lead through **Relationship Building** are the essential glue that holds a team together. Without these strengths on a team, in many cases, the group is simply a composite of individuals. In contrast, leaders with exceptional Relationship Building strength have the unique ability to create groups and organizations that are much greater than the sum of their parts.

Within this domain, a leader with Positivity and Harmony may work hard to minimize distractions and to keep the team's collective energy high. On the other hand, a leader with Individualization might use a more targeted approach to getting people involved. Or a leader with strong Relator or Developer may be a great mentor and guide as he pushes others toward bigger and better achievements.

Leaders with great **Strategic Thinking** strengths are the ones who keep us all focused on what *could be*. They are constantly absorbing and analyzing information and helping the team make better decisions. People with strength in this domain continually stretch our thinking for the future.

Within this domain, a leader using Context or Strategic might explain how past events influenced present circumstances or navigate the best route for future possibilities. Someone with strong Ideation or Input may see countless opportunities for growth based on all of the information she reviews. Or a leader drawing from his Analytical theme might help the team drill into the details of cause and effect.

LEADERSHIP STRENGTHS IN ACTION

In recent years, we have studied leaders who built great schools, created major nonprofit organizations, led big businesses, and transformed entire nations. But we have yet to find two leaders who have the exact same sequence of strengths. While two leaders may have identical expectations, the way they reach their goals is always dependent on the unique arrangement of their strengths.

To help you see how different effective leadership strengths can be, we asked a few of the top organizational leaders we interviewed if they would be willing to share their strengths and their stories. We selected four leaders — one to illustrate each of the four domains of leadership strength. You will notice that these leaders have multiple strengths in the domain they represent.

Throughout the next four sections, you will see how these leaders have leveraged their dominant strengths to drive organizational growth. You will hear from the founder and CEO of one of the most legendary nonprofits of the past century, the president of one of the most respected brands ever, the chairman of one of the world's largest banks, and the chief executive of the largest consumer electronics retailer in the world. As you read each of these stories, you will realize just how different four leaders can be, even at the highest levels of an organization.

EXECUTING

Executing Themes

ACHIEVER	CONSISTENCY	FOCUS
ARRANGER	DELIBERATIVE	RESPONSIBILITY
BELIEF	DISCIPLINE	RESTORATIVE

Wendy Kopp

Founder and CEO
Teach For America

Top Five Strengths

ACHIEVER*

COMPETITION

RESPONSIBILITY*

RELATOR

STRATEGIC

* EXECUTING THEME

During her senior year at Princeton, Wendy Kopp was simply trying to figure out what to do after she graduated. The last thing on Kopp's mind was starting her own business, let alone launching a national movement. Then in late 1988, while seeking a subject for her senior thesis, Kopp found a topic that piqued her interest: educational inequity.

Throughout her time at Princeton, Kopp had noticed two distinct and divergent camps of students, even within that elite institution. One group, composed of students who had attended top-flight East Coast prep schools, often referred to their experience at Princeton as a "cakewalk." The other group, made up of students who had grown up in urban public schools, struggled to meet the academic expectations at the Ivy League university. If it was this bad at Princeton, Kopp thought, then this inequity must be much worse in other parts of the country.

She decided to gather a group of fellow students to discuss the broader problem of why it was so hard for most children to get the education they deserved. When the group convened, she heard student after student express interest in teaching, but she also heard them describe how there was no mechanism for attracting top students to the profession, especially in urban areas that had the most dire need.

It was during this meeting that Kopp's Responsibility theme kicked in. She felt a need to take action, and she started thinking about how she could fix this massive problem. Inspired in large part by the Peace Corps, which was launched by President John F. Kennedy in 1961, Kopp was determined to create a national teacher corps. So, like many idealistic young people, Wendy Kopp wrote a letter to then-President George H.W. Bush, suggesting that he create this new corps. She recommended that recent college graduates commit to two years of teaching in underprivileged areas. Kopp didn't hear back from the White House about her idea.

But it was her next move that truly separated this big idea from the millions of good thoughts that never make it to fruition: the super-achieving, hands-on undergrad decided that she would build this national teacher corps *herself*. In addition to making educational inequity the focus of her senior thesis, Kopp began researching what it would take to create a national corps of teachers. As she was reviewing recommendations that had been made to President Kennedy about what it would take to establish the Peace Corps, she found a paper from one of Kennedy's advisors that suggested that a minimum of 500 people were necessary (on day one) to convey the sense of urgency and national importance. This paper inspired Kopp's incredibly ambitious goal: She would find 500 new corps members in the first year to make her dream of a national teacher corps a reality.

As Kopp began to run the numbers in terms of what it would take to recruit all of these high-achieving students to volunteer for two years, she realized it would require at least $2.5 million, for the first year alone, to get her project off the ground. She knew this was an ambitious goal, but she felt an immediate responsibility to do it. When Kopp mentioned this figure to her thesis advisor, he exclaimed, "Do you know how hard it is to raise twenty-five *hundred* dollars?" Kopp actually didn't know just how hard it would be, but she was about to find out.

Kopp started by building her core team — for recruiting, training, and meeting her aggressive fundraising goal. She enlisted a few of the brightest people she knew, although it took a lot of convincing to get them to commit to this underfunded start-up. Over the next 12 months, Kopp's leadership team went through a series of extraordinary challenges and found themselves on the brink of quitting on several occasions. But great Achievers rarely give up.

To make things even more difficult, while Kopp was serious about starting with 500 teachers, she was not about to accept just anyone who applied. She wanted this new program, dubbed "Teach For America," to be very selective. This meant that the organization had to recruit, interview, and screen more than 2,500 applicants just to get 500 of the best and brightest graduates. Kopp felt that the organization had a responsibility to hire graduates who could have an immediate impact in the schools they joined.

This series of daunting challenges was no match for Wendy Kopp's extraordinary determination and ability to execute. By April of 1990, a year after Kopp graduated from Princeton, the first 500 members of Teach For America gathered for their orientation session at the University of Southern California. Kopp had managed to raise the $2.5 million *and* build the organization from scratch — over the span of a single year.

Then, as if events simply followed the script Kopp had written in her senior thesis, the nation took notice of her bold launch. Her efforts were featured on *Good Morning America* and in *TIME* magazine. A *New York Times* headline read: "Princeton Student's Brainstorm: A Peace Corps to Train Teachers." Teach For America's first year was a remarkable success, but Kopp knew she had a responsibility to keep the organization alive and to prepare it for long-term success.

In 2008, we followed up with Wendy Kopp to see how things were going at Teach For America almost two decades after its inception. Upon entering the organization's New York headquarters, we noted that the offices still had the feel of a small start-up aiming to change the world. The building was abuzz with young people rushing around close quarters and filled with small cubicles and plywood desks. The water heaters in the makeshift restrooms doubled as toilet paper holders. Even in 2008, Teach For America's humble environment certainly didn't convey that of one of the most successful start-ups of the past century.

And when we sat down with Kopp, it was clear that the super achiever remained in overdrive. Kopp was just days away from giving birth to her fourth child, yet she was in the midst of a full day at Teach For America. Although in obvious discomfort, Kopp was not about to slow down. You could tell from the look in her eyes and the passion in her voice that she is never quite content with where things are today.

Kopp described how hard it had been to build an organization that now has a stable — and robust — flow of funding and applicants. She described her most fundamental challenge, quite succinctly, as "finding talent." To keep the organization growing, Kopp had to surround herself with the best teachers, fundraisers, and leaders for the future. In her own words, talent was *the* key element because it "solves all the other problems."

It was clear from our discussion that Kopp had found the right people — not only to expand Teach For America, but also to make an impact on an entire nation. When we asked about the outcomes of all this hard work, Kopp told us that her organization's fundraising goal for the current year was a whopping $120 million. What's more, in the previous year, Teach For America had more than 25,000 applicants and is now regarded as one of the most selective and prestigious jobs in the United States, even for Ivy League graduates. In 2005, one in eight Yale graduates applied for a Teach For America position. Year after year, thousands of students are now passing up six-figure salaries at high-prestige companies such as GE and Goldman Sachs to spend two years teaching in an inner-city school.

Yet what might be an even greater legacy are the future community leaders who emerge among Teach For America's alumni. Many of today's brightest young politicians, businesspeople, and school superintendents got their start in the organization that Kopp built. We interviewed a former member from Washington, D.C., who described how the head of that city's school system and half of her staff were Teach For America alumni. Nevertheless, when we asked Kopp about the leadership legacy she would leave, it was clear she had yet to give the question much thought. Perhaps she was too busy making things happen to wax philosophical.

One of the more revealing questions we asked Kopp was about how she prioritizes her time. She quickly described how she starts each year with a structured list of all the things she needs to accomplish in the next 12 months; then she breaks that list down by month and week. From the weekly list, she creates a daily to-do list that she follows rigorously. As Kopp talked about how she has all of this "systematized," it sounded like she assumed that we all do this. For her, this level of organization is natural. Kopp told us, "I couldn't exist without that — or at least I couldn't be doing this job without that system."

As we listened to Kopp, it was easy to hear how her top five strengths played a role in the remarkable success of Teach For America. When she spoke about all the children who deserve a better education, you could hear how her Responsibility theme motivates her. As one Teach For America alumnus recounted, "Wendy conveys more than her vision for educational equity — the responsibility to do something about it. To simply be the best new teacher isn't enough. Winning for the sake of students is the only option."

And while Kopp's Competition theme wasn't quite evident on the surface, it manifested in the context of "winning" for students in the face of the status quo. For Kopp, her Competition was more organizational and societal than it was personal. She did everything in her power to ensure that the teachers her organization placed in schools were even better than the top teachers hired through the conventional system.

Yet of all the leaders we have studied, Wendy Kopp may be the best example of how you can take one dominant strength, Achiever, and spend a lifetime applying it. From her detailed task lists to building a national movement from scratch in one year, Kopp's ability to make things happen is without parallel. While her organization has already reached more than *three million* students, it is unlikely that she will rest until children around the world have access to the education they deserve.

INFLUENCING

Influencing Themes

ACTIVATOR	COMPETITION	SIGNIFICANCE
COMMAND	MAXIMIZER	WOO
COMMUNICATION	SELF-ASSURANCE	

Simon Cooper

President
The Ritz-Carlton

Top Five Strengths

MAXIMIZER*

WOO*

ARRANGER

ACTIVATOR*

SIGNIFICANCE*

* INFLUENCING THEME

When Simon Cooper assumed his role as president of The Ritz-Carlton Hotel Company in 2001, he faced a unique challenge. Whereas Wendy Kopp essentially had to create an organization from scratch, Cooper's charge was to take one of the world's greatest brands to a new level of excellence. While it's debatable which assignment had a higher degree of difficulty, Cooper clearly had the most to lose.

The Ritz-Carlton brand was already as synonymous with luxury as Kleenex is with tissue. Their employees were satisfied. Customers were engaged. Quality was ingrained in almost every aspect of the business. Expectations were sky high.

And on a more personal level, Cooper was taking over for a charismatic leader, Horst Schulze, who *was* the brand for nearly two decades. According to Cooper, Schulze "walked on water" in the eyes of Ritz-Carlton's people. With this venerable brand firing on all cylinders, Cooper faced a situation in which there was almost nowhere to go but down. But nothing energizes a Maximizer more than the challenge of taking a company from great to world-class.

When you sit in a room with Cooper, you can almost feel the power exuding from his weathered skin. Born just outside of London, Cooper once sailed charter yachts for a living and played competitive rugby until he was 45. It's still easy to see the former athlete in Cooper's stature and build. Yet his voice and accent are as sophisticated as the brand he leads. Until you get to know Simon Cooper, this refinement seems to mask his intensity and confidence.

From the moment Cooper took the helm at Ritz-Carlton in 2001, he was determined to leave his mark. Like many who lead with the Significance theme, the last thing he wanted to do was simply follow in the footsteps of his predecessor. As Cooper reconstructed the situation, he explained how careful he was to be clear from the outset that he was not planning to walk in someone else's shoes. In his mind, this was the one sure kiss of death for anyone entering a new leadership role. Although his predecessor was widely revered, Cooper knew that the last thing people wanted was a pretender leading the organization.

He also realized that the brand had to grow far beyond the personality of its leader.

Instead of trying to remake a brand that was already at a pinnacle, Simon Cooper aimed to broadly expand Ritz-Carlton's global influence. He started by studying exactly what Ritz-Carlton's customers *already* loved, and he then sought to maximize this opportunity. For Cooper, the key was building on the strengths of the brand. He quickly realized that none of his customers truly *needed* to stay at a Ritz-Carlton. They could easily frequent others properties for half the price, yet they continually returned to the Ritz. So Cooper dedicated even more of his time and attention to studying the unique experience that Ritz-Carlton created for its customers.

As Cooper studied his customers' attachment to the brand, he estimated that 90% of its image was emotional — it was how Ritz-Carlton's employees "bring the brand to life" every time they interact with a guest. Cooper described:

People create memories, not things. If we ask guests what color the carpet was in their guest room, they probably won't know. The real value comes from the ladies and gentlemen [employees] *who bring that hotel to life. Ten percent is the platform, but the rest is people.*

Perhaps this is why Cooper finds himself in his element when spending time with Ritz-Carlton's frontline employees. During his visits, one thing Cooper loves to do is ask his associates what their guests like to buy. While he writes down their responses, which usually consist of the room, food service, or spa treatments, Cooper has another lesson in mind. His follow-up question is somewhat unorthodox: "Now tell me what they *can't* buy."

This is what Cooper sees as his company's core value proposition: delivering the intangibles like smiles, relationships, and caring service. In a world where many guests can purchase just about anything they desire, it is the things they *can't* buy that create true engagement with the Ritz-Carlton brand. Cooper described how he compensates his leaders based on their ability to foster this kind of true engagement, instead of basic loyalty, because they are "in the business of trying to win the hearts and minds" of each guest. If they are able to do so, Simon Cooper hopes to leave behind a legacy of what he calls "guests for life."

Once again making the most of his top theme, Maximizer, Cooper was determined to take a legendary guest experience to an entirely different level. Gallup's initial measures of Ritz-Carlton's employee engagement levels placed them in the top quartile of Gallup's worldwide database. But this was nowhere near "good enough" for Ritz's leadership team, who viewed this as a minimum standard. When Gallup audited Ritz-Carlton's customer engagement, they set an even higher bar. While most of their properties are above the 95th percentile in our customer engagement database — a level that most organizations would consider world-class — Ritz-Carlton challenged its properties to be in the 98th to 99th percentile. If they had a property in the

94th or 95th percentile, it was considered to be in the "red" zone. A hotel in the 96th or 97th percentile was classified as "yellow," and a property could only get to "green" when it reached the 98th percentile. When it comes to a guest's engagement with the brand, Cooper and team were determined to set a new gold standard.

The second major initiative Simon Cooper launched was also aimed at creating lifelong guests, albeit in a bit more direct manner. In the face of resistance, Cooper made the case for Ritz-Carlton to move into selling private residences and fractional ownership. When Cooper introduced this concept in 2002, his judgment was called into question by *The Wall Street Journal* and others. They wondered if placing the iconic Ritz-Carlton logo on residences and time shares would dilute the brand. But Cooper would hear nothing of it.

Cooper had more than enough confidence to sell this concept to the world. When questioned in a 2002 interview about the 11 residences atop New York's Battery Park Hotel, Cooper quickly explained how units selling for a minimum of $25 million — which were occupied by high-profile and celebrity types — didn't exactly "hurt the Ritz-Carlton image." By 2008, Ritz-Carlton's residences and clubs (fractional ownership) were the fastest growing segment of the business, with more than 40 new locations planned around the globe. As evidenced by the financial results, this went on to become one of the best business moves in the company's storied history.

A great financial success alone was probably not enough to satisfy Cooper's need to have a significant impression on the world. When we interviewed him in 2008, it was clear that he took even more pride in the global impact of his organization. Cooper casually talked about visits with kings and heads of state as if they were old friends. And he reveled in telling the story of how he asked rock star/philanthropist Bono to join him in a morning meeting with the housekeeping staff during one of his recent stays. You could see how much pride Cooper took in doing little things like this to win others over.

When Cooper steps back and looks at his influence leading Ritz-Carlton, he regards it in a way that may be too big for most chief executives to get their minds around. His influence is not just about maximizing one of the world's greatest brands. Nor is it about doubling the total number of Ritz-Carlton properties in a mere seven years. And it's not just about the records he set in profits, quality, or employee and customer engagement.

Rather, Simon Cooper's talent for influencing serves the greater purpose of running an organization upon which the well-being of more than 40,000 families depends. As Cooper described how the paycheck of one of his frontline employees in Asia often subsidizes the food and shelter for an entire family, you could hear his Significance theme resonate. Then when he talked of the night-and-day difference that a job at Ritz-Carlton could make for a housekeeper in the Persian Gulf, you get a sense that this is one man who realizes that he can change the world — even if that means influencing one person at a time.

RELATIONSHIP BUILDING

Relationship Building Themes

ADAPTABILITY	EMPATHY	INDIVIDUALIZATION
CONNECTEDNESS	HARMONY	POSITIVITY
DEVELOPER	INCLUDER	RELATOR

Mervyn Davies

Chairman
Standard Chartered Bank

Top Five Strengths

ACHIEVER

FUTURISTIC

POSITIVITY*

RELATOR*

LEARNER

* RELATIONSHIP BUILDING THEME

If you try to imagine what the chairman of one of the world's largest banks might look like, Mervyn Davies would fit the bill. With his elegantly tailored suit, wire-rimmed glasses, and athletic build, Davies resembles a polished executive right out of central casting. Yet when you speak to Mervyn Davies and study his track record, it becomes clear that he's nothing like the stereotypical chief executive.

From the day that Davies took over as CEO of Standard Chartered, a bank with more than 70,000 employees spread across 70 countries, he relentlessly went against the grain. Instead of thinking solely about the near term, Davies'

Futuristic theme kept him focused on where world markets would be several years down the road. While all of his competitors were emphasizing the then-lucrative markets in Europe and North America, Davies was more interested in diversifying throughout Africa, India, and the Middle East. When other banks were investing in ways to replace people with technology, Davies wanted to invest *even more* time and money in developing his people.

At almost every turn, Davies was leveraging his Relator theme to build stronger connections throughout the organization. In an era when banking CEOs were overly cautious about what they said, Davies instead opted to overcommunicate whenever possible. And while other chief executives were focused almost exclusively on their bottom lines, Davies was just as concerned with building an organization that had "a heart and a soul."

Before he could run Standard Chartered in such an unconventional way, Davies had to begin his tenure by building an extraordinarily diverse leadership team composed of people with vastly different backgrounds and personalities. Given that his company derived more than 90% of its revenue from emerging international markets, Davies felt that he had no choice but to ensure that the bank's leadership group was as diverse as the customers it served. Acutely aware of his own strengths and limitations, Davies set out to surround himself with people who could do specific things much better than he ever could.

Throughout this process, Davies was very candid about his own personality, even placing a coffee cup with his top five themes — Achiever, Futuristic, Positivity, Relator, and Learner — on his desk. He then spent an extensive amount of time analyzing the strengths and weaknesses of people around him, mapping out how they might fit on different teams. This led to some unorthodox leadership choices early on. Just one month into the job, Davies replaced the existing CFO, who had an extensive accounting background, with a young consultant who had no formal accounting experience. What's more, this consultant was still in his thirties. The people around Davies thought he had gone mad.

Fortunately, Davies made concerted efforts to be candid and to overcommunicate about everything he was doing and why he was doing it. This helped him quickly form relationships with key shareholders, business partners, customers, and employees. Then to communicate with his tens of thousands of employees, Davies tried a bit of everything, from videos and cartoons to countless handwritten notes of recognition. He also created more structured communication programs; he would send regular messages to his top 20, 50, and 150 leaders. Davies then made sure to send monthly e-mail updates to all 75,000 employees around the globe. As a result, Standard Chartered's employees always knew what the boss was thinking.

On more than one occasion, Davies was criticized for being too open with his communication. But this didn't quiet him. On the contrary, when Davies' wife of 29 years had a bout with breast cancer during his time as CEO, he sent a candid e-mail to 400 of his top executives explaining exactly what was going on, how he felt, and how it would change his schedule in the upcoming months. And this was not just because it was about *his* personal life — Davies was also widely known for helping everyone at Standard Chartered put their family first. One long-time colleague described how amazed he was that Davies took so much time from his busy schedule to be there for him during a personal crisis.

Davies' candor extended to what he described as "courageous conversations," or more difficult topics. By his own admission, Davies could be very direct at times and described his style as having an "iron fist and velvet glove." Davies also applied this frankness to describing his own personality and shortcomings. He took ownership for his mistakes, and he talked freely about what went wrong.

As a result of Davies' extraordinary openness, Standard Chartered's employees could see how much he loved the bank, and they knew that his heart was in the right place. This created a culture in which employees took ownership over their work instead of passing along blame. It also led to an unprecedented level of trust in their CEO, as they continued to give Davies latitude when he bucked the conventional wisdom. He built trust through relationships.

In 2008, when we sat down to talk with Mervyn Davies in his London offices, he had just moved on from the CEO position to one of a non-executive chairman of Standard Chartered Bank.

By this time, Davies was a regular on *The Times'* list of the most influential businesspeople, and he was widely revered beyond the business community. At the time of our interview, banks around the world were in a state of crisis. Almost every major financial institution was facing substantial losses. But as *The New York Times* and *The Economist* described, Mervyn Davies had set Standard Chartered up to be about the only bank in the world that was able to *grow* through one of the more difficult economic periods in recent history. It was one of the few shining gems in the financial services sector.

When Davies began to describe the reasons why Standard Chartered had thrived in this market, his jovial tone turned serious. As he spoke of the "real soul" and "wonderful story" of this 150-year-old bank that originated in Calcutta, the passion in his voice turned his fair skin a few shades of red. Davies went on to describe how he had "bet his career" early on by focusing on two key things — people and corporate social responsibility — even though many shareholders couldn't have cared less about either one at the time.

While we would have loved to spend even more time talking to Davies about the latter topic — specifically, his contributions to battling HIV/AIDS and cancer globally — to keep our study focused, we attempted to learn more about how Davies had done such an exceptional job of engaging people. So we asked him more about himself on a personal level.

As he began to describe his own personality, you could tell that he was exceptionally comfortable in his own skin. In

Davies' opinion, the most important aspect of leading is simply knowing oneself. In a matter-of-fact tone, he described how, as a leader, you must "know yourself, know the people around you, and then get on with it."

As simple as this may sound, Davies reported that the way he empowered people at times raised red flags. Early on, when he delegated responsibility to employees who had the right strengths and gave them free rein, others worried that he did not have enough personal involvement in key activities. But placing trust in others to deal with areas in which they had competence freed Davies to spend the majority of his time developing talent and coaching future leaders.

Davies described why he opted to use StrengthsFinder and a strengths-based approach throughout Standard Chartered as part of his plans for developing people. "We try to be a company that focuses on people's strengths and not their weaknesses, and I think that the more people realize what their strengths are, the more they can really focus on those areas and really specialize and develop," he said. Davies then concluded with what could be one of the most succinct summaries of the strengths approach that we've ever heard: "If you focus on people's weaknesses, they lose confidence."

It is clear from the bank's financial results that Davies was able to create a culture that engaged people's strengths on a daily basis. But one of the most telling parts of our interview was when Davies talked about the pride he takes from watching other people learn and grow. When we asked about his greatest satisfaction at work, he quickly replied that he could go on for half an hour describing how rewarding it was to see people around him develop and to share in their success.

Davies then took on a more personal tone, describing how he had both of his children take StrengthsFinder and how differently he had developed each of them based on their natural strengths. It was easy to hear the passion in Davies' thick Welsh accent when he spoke of the young people he has had a chance to mentor. When we asked him to talk more about it, he replied, "I love doing that. I absolutely love it. I love listening to them and, you know, at the end of the day, I talk a lot, but I think the greatest skill you've got in management is listening."

Davies then issued a challenge to any aspiring leader. He explained that the litmus test of a great leader is "whether they can quickly write down on a piece of paper all of the people they have developed." If they can't, then Davies thinks those leaders might just have been in the right place at the right time — accidentally and not by design. Not only can Davies assemble a long list of the people and relationships he has invested in over his 15 years at Standard Chartered, but he also expects his people to be able to do the same.

It was clear from our conversation with Davies that he is a man who is in his element when leading people and building relationships. At one point in our discussion, Davies talked about the way people energize him even more than money. Again, not what you might expect to hear from one of the world's most legendary banking executives. Yet during

Davies' tenure, in addition to all of the international expansion, Standard Chartered Bank's stock price soared, and its market capitalization nearly tripled.

By doing things his own way, Davies not only achieved unparalleled financial results, but he also built an organization in which each of his employees could, as Davies put it, "look back on their careers and realize how much fun they had working for the bank." At every turn, you could see Mervyn Davies' keen strength for relationship building and his relentless positivity about the future.

STRATEGIC THINKING

Strategic Thinking Themes

ANALYTICAL	IDEATION	LEARNER
CONTEXT	INPUT	STRATEGIC
FUTURISTIC	INTELLECTION	

Brad Anderson

Chief Executive Officer
Best Buy

Top Five Strengths

CONTEXT*

IDEATION*

INPUT*

LEARNER*

CONNECTEDNESS

* STRATEGIC THINKING THEME

As you enter Best Buy's corporate headquarters in Minneapolis, you can tell that the company does things a bit differently. The building is modeled after an airport terminal with a massive connecting hub in the middle. This hub is always abuzz with conversations and employees who look like they are genuinely having fun. The environment feels more like a student union on a college campus than a Fortune 500 company's corporate headquarters. At first glance, it is hard to figure out how it would be possible to create this kind of atmosphere, let alone in a company with 150,000 employees.

But when we spent some time with Best Buy CEO Brad Anderson in 2008, it all started to make sense. With his round face, bright eyes, and jovial smile, Anderson certainly doesn't look the part of a chief executive. It's easier to picture him teaching a high school history class than running a shareholder meeting. Very few people radiate this level of warmth and sincerity during an initial introduction. Frontline employees at Best Buy describe Anderson as one of the most approachable people they've met.

As much as Anderson's look and demeanor may not fit the conventional CEO mold, his actions and personality wander even farther off the beaten path. Yet over the last 25 years, Anderson took an unknown regional electronics store and helped make it into the largest consumer electronics retailer in America. The amazing story of his career's trajectory is only overshadowed by the organization's performance during his tenure.

If you look at Anderson's top five themes — Context, Ideation, Input, Learner, and Connectedness — you might expect to find someone who was an exceptional student at a young age. But he was not. Anderson struggled and had poor grades in high school. That is why it was such a surprise when Anderson, and his grades, began to thrive in college. Once he was free to study the topics of his choice, it opened his mind to a world of endless opportunity. Anderson's realization in college — that he could build his life around this innate curiosity and voracious appetite for learning — would prove to be critical throughout his career.

At the age of 24, Anderson joined Sound of Music, a small electronics retailer in Minneapolis, as a sales associate. After a few years, he became a store manager. Anderson was then asked to join the team at its corporate office. By 1983, the company had changed its name to "Best Buy" and had seven stores. The retailer expanded and launched several supercenters over the next few years.

By 1986, Anderson had joined the company's board of directors and was working very closely with the company's legendary founder, Dick Schulze. It was around this time that Anderson, Schulze, and a few others began to question the entire model on which electronics retailers operated: Almost every consumer electronics store paid its salespeople based on a commission of how much they sold.

As a result, when customers walked into almost any music or stereo shop prior to 1990, they were mobbed by pushy salespeople trying to close a deal. What's worse, these commissioned sellers were usually hawking the display models that would put the most cash in their pockets, even though the televisions and stereos were not in stock. When Anderson gathered a focus group of customers and asked them which major electronics retailer they trusted, he recalled how they would simply "break into laughter." People felt less pressure walking across a used car lot in those days.

As Anderson looked at successful retailers in other industries, he noticed very different business models. One of his early cues came from the experience that grocery stores provide, where everyone is free to browse and they know that products will be in stock. Anderson, Schulze, and team wondered if Best Buy could follow a similar model — one that they thought would be much more likely to please the average customer. But there were major obstacles in the way, from the way manufacturers and distributors operated to the expectations of the thousands of people in sales roles.

Anderson and Schulze knew that a decision to follow this new model would send shockwaves through the entire industry. But they also had a hunch that it might be the only way for their company to survive. As Anderson later described to us, "That was a breakthrough moment, and it only happened because the company was going to go out of business if we played by the rules."

So when Anderson and Schulze made the formal recommendation — that Best Buy move away from a commissioned sales model — they faced intense resistance. Even within the company, there were many skeptics. But when people challenged the idea, Anderson would remind them to "think about the next *fifteen* years, not the next *five*."

Based on this idea, Best Buy implemented a new strategy that would forever change the retail sales model. As a result of this shift, customers no longer felt the pressure of salespeople breathing down their necks — and were now filing into Best

Buy stores just to browse. Shortly thereafter, other consumer electronics stores and retailers in other industries followed suit.

Anderson's career continued to advance during this time of transition, and he was named Best Buy's president in 1991. From the day Anderson assumed this leadership role, it was clear he wasn't going to fit anyone's preconceived notions of a top corporate executive. Instead of conforming to the new role, this self-described "odd duck" decided to do things quite differently.

While Wall Street analysts, among others, expected Anderson to take a more conventional approach as Best Buy's new president, that's not what he did. Much to their consternation, Anderson would simply disappear for weeks on end in search of new ideas. Instead of poring through trade or business books, he read everything from *Rolling Stone* to historical biographies. Anderson attended non-electronics conferences in search of bigger ideas. He brought in countless outside experts to challenge Best Buy's thinking. His Ideation, Input, and Learner themes were always at work. By Anderson's own admission, he challenged conventional wisdom to the point where it was "radically complained about by my peers."

Anderson's insatiable curiosity also led to an unconventional people-leadership approach. He quickly surrounded himself with leaders who he knew would challenge his thinking. And he was also careful to select leaders who could effectively develop the strengths of those under their charge. Once again breaking the mold, Anderson was as concerned about the personal chemistry of the team members as he was about their experience or technical competence.

When we spoke with Anderson, he described how his most senior leaders were "wildly different" from one another. Yet they found a way to accommodate each other by placing a great deal of trust in each person's unique strengths. Anderson described how he could talk passionately in an executive meeting about his ideas for the future and turn to see that he had completely lost his CFO's attention. And in turn, when he talked about how his gifted CFO would work through spreadsheets until 8:00 at night, Anderson said, "You might as well give me hieroglyphics." This was just one of the many partnerships Anderson formed to complement his strengths and limitations.

What may be even more remarkable is the degree to which Anderson was able to stay true to his own strengths in his role as CEO. When we asked him how he was able to provide leadership for more than 150,000 Best Buy employees, Anderson described the critical role of his self-awareness and authenticity. While Anderson may not be a natural at working a room or chatting up a store full of frontline employees, he has developed a unique way to connect with Best Buy's employees, customers, and shareholders as he travels around the world: He simply asks great questions.

As one Best Buy employee described, Anderson can walk into a store and make each employee feel like "*the* most important contributor because he asks each person what *they're* doing, what's getting *them* excited, and what *they're* seeing in the store." She went on to describe how she had never seen a CEO do this so well and observed how Anderson is genuinely "curious about people and their own life story." Once he has this context in his mind, it helps him see what needs to happen in the future.

While studying successful leaders like Anderson, one of the most revealing items we asked leaders to respond to was: "Please describe a time when you felt like you were 'in a zone,' where time almost seemed to stand still." Anderson told us that he feels this way almost any time he is learning something, whether it is from a person, a book, or solving a puzzle. He said, "I find it amazing that I can be fifty-eight years old and seem to know less every day. No matter how much you learn, it just continues to open up more substantial questions and relationships."

Anderson went on to tell us about how, the night before our conversation, he had stepped out of a dinner early so he could spend some quality time at a nearby Barnes & Noble before heading home. The voracious learner, who reads several books each week, said that he found at least 28 books he wanted to take home that evening. "It's a disease," he said with a smile.

We suspect that there are millions of Best Buy employees, customers, and shareholders who are glad that Brad Anderson let this lifelong curiosity run its course. While his strategic thinking led to a few experiments that did not pan out, Anderson's unconventional approach helped create unprecedented growth. Had you invested $1,000 in Best Buy's stock in 1991, when Anderson took over as president, it would have been worth $175,000 by 2008. Not bad for a guy who started at the ground level and spent the next 25 years soaring with his strengths.

THE COLLECTIVE TALENT OF A TEAM

As you can hear in the stories of these four leaders, they have exceptional clarity about who they are — and who they are *not*. If any one of them had chosen to spend a lifetime trying to be "good enough" at everything, it's doubtful they would have made such an extraordinary impact. Instead, they've all been wise enough to get the right strengths on their teams, and this has set up their organizations for continuous growth. Unfortunately, very few teams are truly optimized around their strengths.

As we learned from working with the top executive team at Hampton, a U.S.-based hotel chain, once a team understands how to leverage each person's strengths, it quickly finds new ways to drive organizational performance. When we first met with Hampton President Phil Cordell, his company and leadership team appeared to be on the right track. With more than 1,500 locations, Hampton was expanding rapidly and had developed a strong consumer brand. Cordell had a leadership team of extraordinarily talented individuals, each of whom possessed a deep passion about the organization and its brand. His team was innovative, creative, and had an impressive track record. Hampton was already well ahead of its competitors, but Cordell wanted to widen that lead. He also hoped to initiate a major international expansion.

Cordell realized that what got his team to that point would not be sufficient for the future, given his ambitious goals. As we conducted interviews with each member of his core executive group, we discovered that they were fiercely loyal to the brand, eager to drive performance, and had great respect for Cordell as the team's leader. But we also found a few potential land mines. Interestingly, the leadership team's loyalty to Cordell had a major drawback. Team members continually escalated their issues to Cordell for resolution instead of working them out among themselves. This eroded trust among colleagues, and it also meant that Cordell always had to be the one to take action, thus creating a bottleneck and slowing everything down.

Unbeknownst to his team, Cordell spent the vast majority of his day in "response mode." He had no desire to be in the middle of all these discussions, nor did he need to be. This was not just a problem of effective delegation; the main issue was that his team members didn't have strong relationships with each other.

After several discussions with Cordell, it was clear that his aggressive growth plans were going to stretch, if not break, the team. To develop a plan and lay the foundation for international growth, Cordell would need to be absent for significant amounts of time. And the way the team was functioning, it would all but collapse if Cordell was taken out of the equation for prolonged periods. Cordell needed to build a team so strong that it would hardly skip a beat when he was gone.

But to get there, his group needed to confront major issues — one of which was that it was composed of extremely talented individuals who knew how to get things done but who were always "competing to take on more," as one member said. While some of you may be wishing that you had this kind of problem in your workplace, at Hampton, it led to a more divided than collaborative team.

After conducting in-depth interviews with each member of the team, along with looking at a composite of their StrengthsFinder results, it became clear that the team needed to build stronger relationships — and do it quickly — if it wanted to establish trust and meet its ambitious growth plans.

Cordell confronted the team's problems as candidly as possible. When members began to talk openly about their challenges, Cordell bluntly said that they had miles to go in developing a "shared culture." He described how he needed the team to feel comfortable enough to have tough discussions, which were not happening. He called the lack of trust a "deal breaker."

The entire team then spent a great deal of time talking about how it could build stronger relationships and trust. Team members quickly realized that they simply didn't spend enough time together; they were all getting so caught up in trying to handle day-to-day requests that they were too busy to think about the team itself, let alone the future.

They also realized that they needed much clearer expectations to maximize efficiency and avoid overlap. Even more disturbing was that most of the team members reported having problems balancing their workload with their family lives because the environment had become ultra-competitive.

These initial meetings and discussions produced substantial changes. For example, Scott and Kurt, two members of the team who had a knack for building relationships, agreed to dedicate more time to helping strengthen team bonds. Gina passionately described how she could help maximize the strengths of others, on the team and beyond, so they have clear expectations and even more room for growth. Judy decided to leverage her ability to stimulate dialogue and ideas to keep the group focused on the future. During one group meeting, the team created "leadership brand" descriptions that detailed how they planned to leverage their strengths to help the company grow.

Soon after these initial discussions, it was clear that Hampton's leadership team was headed in a very different direction. In meetings, instead of getting defensive when Gina would ask questions, the others knew she was just satisfying her need for input. When Judy started in with a big idea, they knew it was a part of her natural instincts, instead of an annoying challenge to the way they were used to doing things. As a group, they agreed to discuss issues collectively before elevating anything to Cordell. In turn, Cordell committed to "knock down" problems that went to him before going through this process.

Six months after these intensive discussions, the relationships, level of trust, and the leadership team as a whole were thriving. Before these conversations, the team would never have met as a group if its leader couldn't be there. But by this point, thanks in part to Scott taking on the responsibility, the team continued to meet and keep things moving in Cordell's absence. From this strong foundation, the team continued to raise the bar on its own while Cordell focused more time on the international expansion.

The teams we have worked with report gaining the most from regular discussions of each person's strengths in the context of the team and its current goals. As you can see from the Hampton leadership group's experience, whether a team has been together 15 days or 15 years, each person benefits from having a basic understanding of the others' strengths. When teams are able to use a common language of strengths, it immediately changes the conversation, creates more positive dialogue, and boosts the team's overall engagement.

WHAT STRONG TEAMS HAVE IN COMMON

Once you have the right people on your team, it's relatively easy to tell if you're headed in the right direction. Gallup has been studying leadership teams for nearly four decades, and we have witnessed some telltale signs of strong, high-performing teams:

1. **Conflict doesn't destroy strong teams because strong teams focus on results.** Contrary to popular belief, the most successful teams are not the ones in which team members always agree with one another. Instead, they are often characterized by healthy debate — and at times, heated arguments. What distinguishes strong

teams from dysfunctional ones is that debate doesn't cause them to fragment. Instead of becoming more isolated during tough times, these teams actually *gain* strength and develop cohesion.

One reason great teams are able to grow through conflict is because they have a laser-like focus on results. Top teams seek out evidence and data and try to remain as objective as possible. As a result, while people may have different views, they are united in seeking the truth. Team members can argue, but in the end, they are on the same side. In sharp contrast, failing teams tend to personalize disagreement, creating territorial divides that continue to grow.

2. **Strong teams prioritize what's best for the organization and then move forward.** While competition for resources and divergent points of view exist, the best teams are able to keep the larger goal in view. Members of high-performing teams are consistently able to put what's best for the organization ahead of their own egos. And once a decision is made, these teams are remarkably quick to rally around it.

One team we worked with had a long, drawn-out debate over whether they should invest in a major new idea. After months of intense discussion, it would have been easy for John, who technically "lost" the argument, to sit back and sulk after the decision was made. Yet the exact opposite occurred. Like other great team members we have studied, John got over the debate quickly and asked, "What resources do you need from me to make this work?" Once a decision is made, members of great teams rally around to help one another (and the organization) succeed.

3. **Members of strong teams are as committed to their personal lives as they are to their work.** The best teams we studied seemed to live a contradiction. Some of the most productive team members work extreme hours and endure amazing levels of responsibility. They sometimes work 60 hours a week and travel frequently. Yet they consider their lives to be in balance. They seem to have enough time to do the things they want to do with their families. As hard as they work for the company, they seem to bring the same level of energy and intensity to their family, social, and community life.

    When we interviewed Standard Chartered's Mervyn Davies, he told us that he takes as much pride in the amount of time he spends with his wife and two children as he does in his bank's extraordinary performance. While this may seem surprising to an outside observer, Davies described how he strives to dedicate 100% of his attention to his family throughout the weekend. Davies extends this philosophy to all of his bank's employees, always encouraging them to put family first.

Our evidence suggests that the most successful teams have members who are highly engaged in their work *and* highly satisfied with their personal lives. By setting this expectation, which so many others perceive as unattainable, they attract new members who want to do the same. This high level of engagement then sets a powerful example for the entire organization.

4. **Strong teams embrace diversity.** Our work with the leadership teams of some of the most innovative and successful companies in the world reveals a simple truth: Having a team composed of individuals who look at issues similarly, who have been the product of comparable educational backgrounds, and who have experiences with similar track records and approaches is not a sound basis for success.

Earlier, we outlined why leadership teams need a diversity of strengths — ideally, including individuals who demonstrate a balance of strengths in different leadership dimensions. But diversity goes well beyond team strengths. We have also discovered that the most engaged teams welcome diversity of age, gender, and race, while disengaged teams may do the opposite.

For example, Gallup's research revealed that actively disengaged team members are 33% more likely to plan on leaving their job if they have a manager of a different race (when compared to having a manager of the same race). However, when we study engaged teams, people are actually a bit *more likely to stay* with the company if they have a manager of a different race. So whereas a disengaged employee is more likely to quit his job if he has a supervisor of another race, an engaged employee is less likely to leave under the same circumstances.

The most engaged teams look at individuals through the lens of their natural strengths, not at physical characteristics. This keeps the team focused on the potential within each person and minimizes the influence of superficial barriers.

5. **Strong teams are magnets for talent.** Another way to spot a strong team is to look for the teams that everyone wants to be on. For some people, it may be hard to understand why anyone would want to join a team that works longer and harder and that comes complete with sky-high expectations. This is especially true when these "it" teams are characterized by intense competition and extreme accountability for results.

    Yet despite all the consequences and pressure, it is your potential stars who most want to be on these teams. They see top teams as the most stimulating place to be — the place where they can demonstrate their leadership and have a real impact. Instead of being intimidated by the challenge and responsibility, they seek out these teams.

As former United Nations Secretary-General Kofi Annan described in a leadership interview with Gallup, building a strong team within an organization requires the same basic ingredients of a successful soccer squad. Annan encourages the teams to "play in a coordinated manner," but he is quick to point out that should not exclude "individual brilliance." Annan explains that as long as the brilliant ones are pulling with us toward the same goal, this individual talent actually strengthens the collective team. As a result, successful teams often have an organization-wide influence.

Building a strong team requires a substantial amount of time and effort. Getting the right strengths on the team is a good starting point, but it is not enough. For a team to create sustained growth, the leader must continue to invest in each person's strengths and in building better relationships among the group members. When leaders can do this, it allows the entire team to spend even more time thinking about the needs of the people they serve.

PART THREE:

UNDERSTANDING WHY PEOPLE FOLLOW

The most effective leaders rally a broader group of people toward an organization's goals, mission, and objectives. They lead. People follow. Yet rarely do we examine *why* people follow. A majority of the research that has been conducted about leadership over the years — including Gallup's work in this area — could be missing one obvious point: You are a leader only if others follow. Leaders are only as strong as the connections they make with each person in their constituency, whether they have one follower or one million. *Yet we continue to focus on leaders and all but ignore their impact on, and the opinions of, the people they lead.*

One problem is that we have studied leaders in isolation from the connections that make them great. As legendary investor Warren Buffett put it, by definition, "A leader is someone who can get things done *through* other people." So while a leader's opinions may be interesting to study, that might not be the right unit of measurement for understanding why a person follows one leader and ignores another.

If you wanted to know why the president of the United States was making a difference in the lives of the American public, would you look to him for the best answers — or would you ask his constituents? When companies want to know why a product is popular, they ask their customers. So, if we want to know why people rally behind a leader, shouldn't we ask *them* why they follow — or how a great leader has improved their lives? If you want to lead, it is critical to know what the people around you need and expect from you.

WHY DO PEOPLE FOLLOW?

To explore why people follow, Gallup conducted a formal study from 2005-2008. Our goal was to obtain the average person's opinion about leadership — instead of experts, historians, CEOs, celebrities, and politicians defining leadership for them. In sharp contrast to other leadership research, which is primarily based on case studies, interviews, research with one organization, or convenience samples, this study looked at a true random sampling of more than 10,000 followers who were contacted via The Gallup Poll. (See Additional Resources section.) This allowed our team to examine leadership that extends beyond an organization's walls — leadership that is taking place in social networks, schools, churches, and families.

After conducting preliminary testing with several questions, we decided to anchor our research around the following key question:

> *What leader has the most positive influence in your daily life? Take a few moments to think about this question if you need to. Once you have someone in mind, please list his or her initials.*

If they listed someone, we followed up with this item:

Now, please list three words that best describe what this person contributes to your life.

    a. _____

    b. _____

    c. _____

Every word in this question was selected with extreme care. The first part forced each person to identify a specific "leader" who "has the most positive influence" in his or her daily life. The word *positive* was included to ensure that we were not studying leaders who have a predominantly negative influence. As Peter Drucker said, "The three greatest leaders of the 20th century were Hitler, Stalin, and Mao. If that's leadership, I want no part of it."

After identifying a leader in the first part of this question, each person was asked to list three words to describe *what the leader contributes to the follower's life.* This allowed our team to collect thousands of followers' open-ended responses, in contrast to asking them to select from categories based on theory, which would bias their responses. Instead of listing categories such as "vision" or "purpose" — which receive a lot of attention in the field of leadership study — we were determined to let the followers define how leaders make a difference . . . *in their own words.*

Upon completion of our initial surveys, we studied the 25 most commonly mentioned words. To our surprise, many of the "usual suspects" like *purpose, wisdom, humor,* and *humility* were nowhere near the top of the list.

As we continued to review the descriptors, distinct patterns started to emerge. In some cases, more than 1,000 people had listed the exact same word, without any categories or options provided. Given that there are more than 170,000 words in the English language, this was impressive. It seems that followers have a very clear picture of what they want and need from the most influential leaders in their lives: trust, compassion, stability, and hope.

Followers' Four Basic Needs
TRUST
COMPASSION
STABILITY
HOPE

TRUST

One of the leaders we interviewed said, "The truth is your bond — you die keeping your promises. If you send the message that your word is not worth much, you'll be paid back on that." As various political and business scandals have illustrated, followers will not tolerate dishonesty. At any level, whether you are a manager, CEO, or head of state, trust might be the "do or die" foundation for leading.

The followers we surveyed also cited *honesty, integrity*, and *respect* as distinct contributions from the leaders in their lives. A serious breach in honesty can destroy a sitting president, the CEO of a major corporation, a friendship, or a marriage. At a less extreme level, people we have interviewed often speak about the way honesty, trust, and respect also serve as basic relationship filters that help them determine whom to spend time with in the workplace.

Gallup's latest research on trust in leadership also suggests that this foundation is closely linked to employee engagement in an organization. One of our national polls revealed that *the chances of employees being engaged at work when they do not trust the company's leaders are just 1 in 12*. In stark contrast, the chances of employees being engaged at work are better than 1 in 2 if they trust the organization's leadership — a more than *sixfold* increase.

Trust also increases speed and efficiency in the workplace. When two people working on a project do not know each other well, it takes a considerable amount of time for them to be able to collaborate productively. There can be a long getting-to-know-you period — a time during which two people warily look each other over. If you're unfamiliar with a colleague, it can take a while to get accustomed to her work style and personality.

Once a basic level of trust is established between two people, they can make things happen in a fraction of the time that it takes other colleagues who don't have that bond. Trust allows people to skip most of the formality and immediately get to what is most important. As Kofi Annan explained, "If you don't have relationship, you start from zero each time."

When you read organizations' mission statements, you'll notice that many of them espouse integrity, trust, and honesty. Who could argue — they speak to basic human ethics and explain how we build lasting relationships. Best Buy's Brad Anderson described trust as "the most cherished and valuable commodity in a work environment."

To learn more about this fundamental leadership need, we have been asking thousands of leaders this question for many years: *"How do you convince a person of your honesty?"* While one might expect a great leader to have an insightful answer to this question, the best leaders actually do not. Instead, they have a surprising, visceral, and almost hostile reaction to being asked. Top leaders often spout a response along the lines of "I just am," or, as one leader put it, "People just know. They see my behavior over time, and they know they can depend on me." Brad Anderson's key to building trust is being authentic, even if that means letting people see his flaws. As a leader, he feels no choice but to be very candid — even when delivering difficult news — because that is the only way to build trust.

Respect, integrity, and honesty are the outcomes of strong relationships built on trust. They don't have to be discussed — just as top leaders know they should not have to waste time convincing someone of their honesty. Likewise, one of the most striking observations from our research on teams was how *little* successful teams talked about trust. On the contrary, the topic of trust *dominated* the discussions of struggling teams. This speaks to the fundamentals of how relationships develop in thriving organizations. Relationship flat-out trumps competence in building trust.

COMPASSION

Unfortunately, most leaders are hesitant to show genuine compassion for the people they lead, at least in the same way they would with a friend or family member. But the results of our studies suggest that it might be wise for these leaders to take a lesson from great managers, who clearly *do* care about each of their employees.

Caring, friendship, happiness, and *love* were other frequently mentioned words followers used when asked what leaders contribute to their lives. These words were not that surprising; Gallup has accumulated a mountain of evidence over the years on the impact of a caring manager. We have asked more than 10 million people to respond to the item "My supervisor, or someone at work, seems to care about me as a person." And we found that people who agree with this statement:

- are significantly more likely to stay with their organization

- have much more engaged customers

- are substantially more productive

- produce more profitability for the organization

Obviously, a major challenge for organizational leaders is that it is difficult to establish close relationships throughout an organization with thousands of employees. When we asked followers more specifically about the "organizational leaders" and "global leaders" that have a positive influence, we found that people expect more general positive energy and "compassion" from high-level organizational/global leaders — compared to much more intimate words (like *caring*) that followers used to describe their everyday leaders.

Or as Standard Chartered's Mervyn Davies explained, organizational leaders must have "a positive bias" because employees simply "don't want to follow negative people around." On a personal level, Davies' compassion was always shining through to Standard Chartered's employees. In addition to being very open with his own challenges as his wife battled breast cancer, Davies was just as concerned about his employees' mental and physical health. He initiated several programs aimed at helping employees boost their overall well-being, and he always encouraged his direct reports to put their family first. He knew that for people to truly love their organization, it needed to have a heart.

STABILITY

Followers want a leader who will provide a solid foundation. They reported that the best leaders were the ones they could always count on in times of need. The people we surveyed also mentioned the words *security*, *strength*, *support*, and *peace*. As a leader, your followers also need to know that your core values are stable. This will buffer them from unnecessary change and ensure that they know what is expected.

Our need for stability and security plays into nearly every decision we make. Politicians work tirelessly to convince us that we will be more secure if they are elected. Spiritual leaders are often great promoters of stability, as followers turn to their messages for strength in times of crisis or elation. Great teachers who lead in classrooms every day know the value of giving students constant support and reassurance.

In the workplace, while it's critical for organizations to evolve, change, and grow over time, they must also offer employees stability and confidence. At a very basic level, employees need a paycheck, and they need to feel secure about having a job. If managers and leaders do not meet these basic needs, they are sure to face resistance. Employees who have high confidence in their company's financial future are *nine times* as likely to be engaged in their jobs when compared to those who have lower confidence about their organization's financial future.

When we spoke with Ritz-Carlton President Simon Cooper, it was clear that he viewed putting food on the table for families around the world as one of the most important elements of his job. He was as concerned about the general well-being of his hourly employees in Jakarta as he was about his wealthy guests. When it came time to think about expansion, Cooper was careful not to add new jobs that would have to be cut soon thereafter if there was an economic downturn.

At a company-wide level, nothing creates stability as quickly as transparency. Followers need to have a basic sense of confidence about where their career is headed and how the organization is doing financially. At a large engineering company we worked with, all of the organization's data and financial metrics, with the exception of payroll information, are easily accessible to everyone in the company. They also provide employees with regular updates on progress toward organizational goals. And perhaps most importantly, leaders throughout the company help each employee see how he or she can directly affect the organization's key metrics like costs, profits, and sales. This gives employees stability and confidence and clears the way for rapid growth.

HOPE

This higher level need poses an interesting challenge; it appears that followers want stability in the moment *and* hope for the future. Followers also mentioned the words *direction*, *faith*, and *guidance* when describing this basic need.

When Gallup studied the impact that leaders can have throughout an organization, the single most powerful question we asked employees was whether their company's leadership made them "feel enthusiastic about the future." Sixty-nine percent of employees who strongly agreed with this statement were engaged in their jobs, compared to a mere 1% of employees who disagreed or strongly disagreed. Based on these data, it appears that this may be the one area in which higher level leaders can have the most influence in their organization.

Instilling hope may seem like an obvious requirement for leading other people. Hope gives followers something to look forward to, and it helps them see a way through chaos and complexity. Knowing that things can and will be better in the future is a powerful motivator. When hope is absent, people lose confidence, disengage, and often feel helpless.

This makes the role of an organizational leader even more important during difficult times. And yet the vast majority of leaders we interviewed did *not* spend enough time deliberately creating more hope and optimism for the future. Instead, even the highest level executives reported that they spend almost all of their time *reacting* to the needs of the day instead of *initiating* for the future.

Whether they realize it or not, leaders who are always reacting convey to the organization that they aren't in charge or control but are being tossed about by the demands of the day. When leaders instead choose to initiate, the very act can create hope for the future. In response to a major economic downturn, one corporate chief we worked with confronted this leadership challenge head-on. In an address to thousands of his employees, he refused to "react to this downturn by cutting spending or laying people off." Instead, he described how the company planned to "gun it" by hiring even more people than planned and by pursuing new areas of business even more aggressively. This kind of initiating creates hope and eliminates helplessness.

In our research, we regularly ask leaders if they spend more time *initiating* or *responding*. While leaders are more likely to claim that they initiate, in reality, they spend the vast majority of their time responding. As part of this research, we provided leaders with several scenarios to prioritize, and in most cases, the leaders we studied did not choose the one option (out of four) that involved initiating. Instead, their priorities were always dominated by a visceral need to respond. Even when we prompted leaders beforehand by asking if they spend more time initiating or responding, it seems that leaders couldn't help but be reactive.

One challenge is that our ability to progress in our career is often determined by our effectiveness in responding to near-term needs. When high value is placed on solving these kinds of problems, it creates a culture in which leaders spend little or no time thinking about what *could* be done because they receive more accolades for simply doing what *needs* to be done.

Another reason we get caught in perpetual response mode is because it's easier. Agreeing to take on a small objective —

for example, cleaning out your inbox by the end of each day — is much more manageable than embarking on a larger and more proactive goal — like creating a new product or mapping out how to double your business in three to five years. Solving problems and removing barriers comes naturally to many people, while initiating is much harder work.

While solving difficult problems is an essential part of effective leadership, identifying opportunities for the future plays a much more important role in creating hope and optimism. As Teach For America's Wendy Kopp demonstrated, it took a big vision and her activation of that idea to offer hope to thousands of teachers, students, and an entire nation. "What I learned, in essence, was that if I was to fulfill my mission, it would take more than an idealistic vision," Kopp wrote in her book. "In the end, the big idea was important and essential. But it would work only with a lot of attention to the nuts and bolts of effective execution."

One of the greatest challenges for leaders is to initiate new efforts that will create subsequent organizational growth. If as a leader, you are not creating hope and helping people see the way forward, chances are, no one else is either.

LEADERSHIP THAT LASTS *BEYOND* A LIFETIME

When we invest our financial resources, we understand that it's best to bet on winning funds, stocks, and companies. Most of us know better than to sink all of our money into a business that has consistently struggled. Yet when we think about how to invest our personal resources, we continue to put more time and energy into perennial losers. Instead of honing our natural strengths, we strive to fill in what nature left out.

The most effective leaders know better than to try to be someone they are not. Whenever they spot an opportunity, they reinvest in their strengths. Wendy Kopp kept on achieving, just as Brad Anderson continued to paint new pictures of the future. With this acute awareness of their strengths and limitations, these leaders were able to partner with the right people to create unprecedented growth.

Leaders stay true to who they are — and then make sure they have the right people around them. Those who surround themselves with similar personalities will always be at a disadvantage in the long run to those who are secure enough in themselves to enlist partners with complementary strengths. As you could hear from the leaders we interviewed, they were always looking for people who could do specific things much *better* than they ever could.

The most effective leaders also get people to follow. Reaching the level where your life's work and mission continue in perpetuity requires not only being a leader yourself, but developing the people who follow you to be effective leaders as well. As Standard Chartered Chairman Mervyn Davies put it, unless you can, on command, write down a list of the people you have developed, you may just be in a leadership position by accident. This is why Davies challenges all of his direct reports to list the people they have developed, and he expects them to ask the same of the people they lead. He understands that the only way to have a broad impact is to create a network of strong leaders that begins to grow on its own.

Perhaps this is why the most extraordinary leaders do not see personal success as an end in itself. They realize that their impact on this world rests in the hands of those who follow. Martin Luther King Jr. preached on the evening of April 3, 1968, "I may not get there with you. But I want you to know tonight that we, as a people, will get to the Promised Land." The next day, Dr. King was assassinated. Yet his influence on the world had just begun.

The day after his death, millions already stood on King's shoulders. By the turn of the 20th century, that number had increased to hundreds of millions. At the end of this century, whether they realize it or not, billions will lead better lives due to Dr. King's efforts during his all-too-brief 39 years.

Perhaps the ultimate test of a leader is not what you are able to do in the here and now — but instead what continues to grow long after you're gone.

ADDITIONAL RESOURCES

TAKING STRENGTHSFINDER

As human beings, we have vast individual differences, and leaders are no exception. The best leaders have an acute awareness of their natural strengths — and their limitations. They understand where to invest their time to get the greatest return on their strengths. And they know the areas where they lack natural talent and need to reach out to others.

To help you build on your strengths and the strengths of the people around you, we have included access to a leadership-specific version of the Clifton StrengthsFinder program with this book. You may be familiar with StrengthsFinder from the bestsellers *Now, Discover Your Strengths*; *StrengthsFinder 2.0*; or a host of other popular books that feature the assessment. Over the past decade, this assessment has helped millions of people in more than 50 countries discover and describe their strengths.

In the back of this book, you will find a packet with a unique access code that will enable you to take the latest version (2.0) of StrengthsFinder. Upon completion of the assessment, you will receive a highly customized Strengths-Based Leadership Guide that lists your top five themes of strength as well as several suggestions for leading with each theme and illustrations of each theme in action. (If you have already taken StrengthsFinder, you can log on to the website using this new code; follow the instructions to receive the new leadership guide based on your existing results.)

In the next section of this book, for each of the 34 themes, you will find a brief definition of the theme, strategies for leveraging that theme to meet followers' four basic needs, and tips for leading *others* who are strong in that theme. While the guide you receive online will be more customized to your strengths, the sections that follow can be used as a reference for building on the strengths of your team and the people around you.

Leading with Your Strengths:
A Guide to the 34 Themes

34 StrengthsFinder Themes

ACHIEVER	FUTURISTIC
ACTIVATOR	HARMONY
ADAPTABILITY	IDEATION
ANALYTICAL	INCLUDER
ARRANGER	INDIVIDUALIZATION
BELIEF	INPUT
COMMAND	INTELLECTION
COMMUNICATION	LEARNER
COMPETITION	MAXIMIZER
CONNECTEDNESS	POSITIVITY
CONSISTENCY	RELATOR
CONTEXT	RESPONSIBILITY
DELIBERATIVE	RESTORATIVE
DEVELOPER	SELF-ASSURANCE
DISCIPLINE	SIGNIFICANCE
EMPATHY	STRATEGIC
FOCUS	WOO

LEADING WITH ACHIEVER

People strong in the Achiever theme have a great deal of stamina and work hard. They take great satisfaction from being busy and productive.

BUILD TRUST

❑ Others respect your work ethic and dedication. Hard work and productivity are visible signs that you are someone who can be trusted to do things right. Live up to that trust. Deliver when you say you will.

❑ Establish relationships with others by working alongside them. Working hard together can be a bonding experience. When others see that you're willing to put your shoulder to the wheel and work beside them, you'll make a connection. Showing people that you see yourself as an equal, not a superior, can inspire feelings of trust and respect.

SHOW COMPASSION

❑ Because setting and achieving goals is of paramount importance to you, apply this way of living to more areas. Not spending enough time with the significant people in your life? Choose someone you care about, take on a project that both of you would like to accomplish, and set a timeline. You'll feel good about what you get done and about the time you spend together.

❑ Every day, put at least one personal relationship goal on your list of things to do. You'll make people feel worthy of your time and investment — plus you'll have the satisfaction of checking the "done" box daily.

PROVIDE STABILITY

❑ Others can count on your belief in the importance of hard work and diligent effort, and they come to expect this from you. They see your consistency and effort as an example of what it takes to create a steady, secure life, and this gives them a sense of stability. Talk to people about how it feels to always give everything you have. Strive to help them see that the one thing they can control in life is their own effort.

❑ Your stamina causes others to see you as a "rock." You are always working; you never seem to tire. People may even feel sorry for you because you put in such long hours. Gently explain to these people that while others may not work this way, it's what feels good to you. Ask them what makes them feel good about their approach to work. Strive to understand and support others by giving them confidence in their own approach to their work.

CREATE HOPE

❑ Your tremendous energy and desire to accomplish as much as possible serves as an inspiration to others. You can encourage people by knowing what they want to accomplish and asking about their progress. By helping others put together timelines and checklists, you can help them achieve their plans and dreams.

❑ Setting goals and deadlines, so motivating for you, can also help others manage massive projects they undertake. You can make a large, complicated endeavor seem manageable by breaking it down and creating milestones along the way. When someone seeks you out for guidance about a colossal task, share your systems for managing the whole in a piece-by-piece manner.

LEADING *OTHERS* WITH STRONG ACHIEVER

❑ When you have projects that require extra work, call on this person. Remember that the saying "If you want to get a job done, ask a busy person" is generally true.

❑ Recognize that this person likes to be busy. Sitting in meetings is likely to be very boring for him. So either let him get his work done or arrange to have him attend only those meetings where you really need him and he can be fully engaged.

❑ Help this person measure what he gets done. He may enjoy keeping track of hours, but more importantly, he should have a way to measure cumulative production. Simple measures such as number of customers served, customers known by name, files reviewed, prospects contacted, or patients seen will help give him definition.

❑ Establish a relationship with this person by working alongside him. Working hard together is often a bonding experience for people with strong Achiever talents. And keep low producers away from him. He's annoyed by "slackers."

❑ When this person finishes a job, a rest or an easy assignment is rarely the reward he wants. He will be much more motivated if you give him recognition for past achievement and then a new goal that stretches him.

❑ This person may well need less sleep and get up earlier than most. Look to him when these conditions are required on the job. Also, ask him questions such as "How late did you have to work to get this done?" or "When did you come in this morning?" He will appreciate this kind of attention.

❑ You may be tempted to promote this person simply because he is a self-starter. This may be a mistake if it leads him away from what he does best. A better course would be to pinpoint his other themes and strengths and look for opportunities for him to do more of what he already does well.

LEADING WITH ACTIVATOR

People strong in the Activator theme can make things happen by turning thoughts into action. They are often impatient.

BUILD TRUST

- ❏ Action is what you are all about. Show people that you are someone whose ideals and principles are not just talk. Do something that promotes the values that are important to you. Make a difference. Demonstrate your integrity. Make your actions a reflection of your words.

- ❏ Action for action's sake is not enough. Honoring the desires of others is a way of demonstrating respect. Is this the direction they want to take? Are they willing to carry out what you start? Making certain that you are truly on their side, not merely promoting your own agenda, will build the trust and respect that allow you to lead.

SHOW COMPASSION

- ❏ Activator talents can be a catalyst for creating one-on-one relationships and then taking them to the next level. Is there someone you can help? Reach out and offer. Make the first move, and you can boost the number of people in your network or deepen a connection that leads to an important friendship.

- ❏ Your rapid actions, on behalf of another person, send a powerful message. By showing that you care, you can create bonds much more rapidly than idle words.

PROVIDE STABILITY

- ❏ Stability may not be the first thing that comes to mind when thinking about activation. However, consistency is part of stability — and you are consistently there to help others overcome hurdles and blast through resistance. Say it out loud: Let others know that you enjoy moving an objective forward and breaking bottlenecks. Knowing that you are there as a resource is a comfort to people who lack your talent for action.

☐ Perhaps courage is the part of stability you can offer. When others are reluctant to act and know they can count on you to help push them or their idea forward, they feel a sense of confidence that they do not have to go it alone. They can count on you to get them there faster.

CREATE HOPE

☐ You can help others by reducing their fear of failure. "You never know until you try" is an Activator attitude. Your ability to boost people's belief in a positive outcome and reduce the trepidation of a negative one can be very productive. "What's the worst case scenario?" you might ask. Helping others see that even the downside isn't so terrifying can be one way to lead them and help move them toward their dreams sooner than they would have gotten there without you.

☐ Sometimes others simply need your energy to move them from fear to action. Getting started can be daunting, especially when uncertainty looms. Your "put one foot in front of the other" approach can help lessen the intimidation factor. Boost others' confidence that they can launch initiatives and new projects. Cheer them on by sharing your enthusiasm, and help them gain momentum.

LEADING *OTHERS* WITH STRONG ACTIVATOR

☐ Give this person the responsibility for initiating and organizing a project that fits within her area of expertise.

☐ Tell this person that you know she is someone who can make things happen and that you will be asking her for help at key times. Your expectations will energize her.

☐ Assign this person to a team that is bogged down and talks more than it performs. She will stir them into action.

❑ When this person complains, listen carefully — you may learn something. Then get her on your side by talking about new initiatives that she can lead or new improvements that she can make. Do this immediately, because unchecked, she can quickly stir up negativity when she gets off track.

❑ Examine this person's other dominant themes. If she is strong in Command, she may have the potential to sell and persuade very effectively. If she is also strong in Relator or Woo, she may become an excellent recruiter for you, drawing in recruits and then pressing them to commit.

❑ To prevent this person from running into too many obstacles, partner her with people who are strong in Strategic or Analytical. They can help her look around the corner. However, you may have to intercede for her in these partnerships so that her instinct to act is not stymied by their desire to discuss and analyze.

LEADING WITH ADAPTABILITY

People strong in the Adaptability theme prefer to "go with the flow." They tend to be "now" people who take things as they come and discover the future one day at a time.

BUILD TRUST

❑ Sometimes all you can do is help people learn to trust themselves and find their own ability to cope. When others feel like their power over a situation is lost, you can help them see that they still create the outcome by how they react. By trusting in their ability and helping them believe in what they can do, you can give them confidence in themselves.

❑ You don't grab the reins and try to take control. Rather, you are a co-traveler on the road of life. Your very lack of a personal agenda helps others come to trust that you are truly there to participate with, rather than manipulate, them. Ask questions about where people want to go, and help them get there. They will know that you are truly on their side.

SHOW COMPASSION

❑ Others have such an appreciation for the way you are "in the moment" when you are together. Make it a priority to focus on them — their feelings, their needs. Things may change in the future, but where they are right now is real. You can honor that and make them feel special by focusing your attention on what is important to them when you spend time together.

❑ Your ability to go with the flow creates a certain freedom from anxiety and allows frustrations to become more fleeting. This is good medicine for a number of other talent profiles. When others get stressed out, you're able to put things in perspective. Help others find the comfort that comes from releasing a need to control every aspect of life. Free them to be happier, whatever the circumstances might be.

❏ Responding to the task at hand is one of your great gifts. Your awareness of the immediate situation and attentiveness to others can't help but make them feel cared for. Sometimes you lead by responding to people's emotional states and helping them sort through what they require. This makes you an important partner when others are in need.

PROVIDE·STABILITY

❏ Stability and flexibility — do they mix? Sure. Consider the jointed palm tree with a segmented trunk that makes it strong enough to withstand gale-force winds. In much the same way, you help others feel safe and secure by your lack of rigidity. When their plans have been carefully laid out, they may be thrown off course by a bump in the road or a detour. You can help them see that these "side roads" are sometimes the necessary, even preferred, paths to ultimate success. Help them "hang in there" when obstacles threaten plans. Show them that they can navigate the next part of the journey.

❏ Patience is a virtue, but you may need to remind others of that from time to time. Those who need fast action and results may give up too easily and not persevere for the long haul. You can provide comfort and refuge by encouraging them to relax and let nature take its course. The resulting outcome may be better than anything they could have artificially orchestrated.

CREATE HOPE

❏ Give others the permission they may need to stop controlling and start living. Inspire them by sharing your perspective, experience, and wisdom.

❏ Acceptance is very likely something you have to offer. Once an event, good or bad, is in the past, how can you help others cope and move beyond it? Think of the times you've come to terms with something you could not control. How did you feel? What did you do? Can you help others do the same?

LEADING *OTHERS* WITH STRONG ADAPTABILITY

❑ This person lives to react and respond. Position him so that his success depends on his ability to adjust to the unforeseen and then run with it.

❑ Let this person know about the plans you're making, but unless he is also strong in Focus, don't expect him to do the planning with you. He is likely to find much preparation work boring.

❑ Examine this person's other dominant themes. If he also has strong talents in Empathy, you might try to position him in a role in which he can be sensitive to and accommodate the varied needs of customers or guests. If one of his other strong themes is Developer, cast him in a mentor role.

❑ Be ready to excuse this person from meetings about the future, such as goal-setting meetings or career-counseling sessions. He is a "here and now" person and will find these meetings rather irrelevant.

LEADING WITH ANALYTICAL

> People strong in the Analytical theme search for reasons and causes. They have the ability to think about all the factors that might affect a situation.

BUILD TRUST

❏ Think about what you endorse. Because others trust your analytical mind, they may follow your recommendations without investigation of their own. This may be just fine, but at times, others may need your help to realize that what's right for you may not be what's right for them. Help them sort out the factors that make an action or product likely to be successful for their individual needs and desires rather than allowing them to base their analysis on yours. Help them know that you want what's best for them, and they will trust you even more.

❏ You automatically uncover what's real, true, and honest. Others will count on you to be the "truth finder" in any information that may conflict or confuse. Think of this as a way you can support others, and don't wait for them to ask for help. Extend yourself; they will respect and trust your proactive analysis.

SHOW COMPASSION

❏ Others who love to scrutinize ideas will be drawn to your analytical, truth-seeking approach. Stimulate debates, the tug-of-war of ideas that challenge one another. Make it fun to explore new ideas and sort out what is fact and what is conjecture. When you find a kindred spirit, take a gamesman's approach to discussion and debate, and forge a relationship that you will both enjoy.

❏ Responding to people in crisis is an obvious way to extend compassion and caring. When others are overwhelmed by data and decisions, you can step in to help sort what's real and what can improve their odds in a difficult situation.

PROVIDE STABILITY

❑ Data are a source of security for many people; if the research backs it, then they are willing to accept a plan and its consequences. Because you carefully examine all possibilities and non-possibilities, you provide the sense of security that many people seek. Do your homework carefully, and know that others are looking to follow your lead.

❑ Your endorsement can be a source of confidence that allows others to trust their own judgment. Thus empowered, they can move forward and make things happen. When you believe others are making good decisions, tell them. Your belief in their opinions and reasoning can give them the certainty and strength they need to proceed.

CREATE HOPE

❑ Cheer for others when they are doing something difficult that you believe is right. They may be trying to guess how you feel or what you would do. Give praise for wise judgment, and offer encouragement that they can face what's ahead. If you believe they will be successful, tell them.

❑ If others seek you out for advice in making decisions, offer to break down your thought process, and show them how it helps you sort information. Be aware that many people may not be capable of following suit. However, some will want to be students of your approach. Though it may be so well-practiced that it's automatic for you, try to articulate the steps you use for analysis. If you have a willing student, teach.

❑ Guidance can be a mutual endeavor. Partner with someone who has action-oriented talents. You can help them make wise, considered decisions. They can help you turn your analysis into action. Both of you will benefit and be inspired to grow.

LEADING *OTHERS* WITH STRONG ANALYTICAL

❏ If you are explaining a decision that has already been made to this person, remember to lay out the logic of the decision very clearly. To you, it may feel as though you are overexplaining things, but for her, this level of detail is essential if she is to commit to the decision.

❏ Every time you have the opportunity, recognize and praise this person's reasoning ability. She is proud of her disciplined mind.

❏ Remember that this person has a need for exact, well-researched numbers. Never try to pass shoddy data to her as credible evidence.

❏ Discovering patterns in data is a highlight in this person's life. Always give her the opportunity to explain the pattern in detail to you. This will be motivational for her and will help solidify your relationship.

❏ You will not always agree with this person, but always take her point of view seriously. She has probably thought through her points very carefully.

LEADING WITH ARRANGER

People strong in the Arranger theme can organize, but they also have a flexibility that complements this ability. They like to figure out how all of the pieces and resources can be arranged for maximum productivity.

BUILD TRUST

- ❏ You want people to tell you the truth because you depend on honest feedback to make important midcourse corrections if necessary. Make sure people know that you expect the truth and that they will not be penalized for telling you exactly what they are thinking. Likewise, foster mutual respect by being honest with them.

- ❏ When you create new systems, plans, or ways to execute, do so with extreme transparency. Being very open about your thought process will help people understand and follow your reasoning.

SHOW COMPASSION

- ❏ When you invest your time considering what's right for other people and how to position them for success, they can't help but love you for it. You may see far more clearly than they do what they can do easily and well. Tell them what you see, and give them "permission" to be who they are and to do what they do best. You will free them to have a more satisfying life if you can minimize the frustrations and maximize the joys.

- ❏ Sometimes others simply need you to come to the rescue. Overwhelmed with confusion and dissonance, they may be rendered emotionally helpless. When you see someone going into overload, step in and help her simplify her world. Show her how all the pieces can be arranged to fit together — and reduce the chaos.

PROVIDE STABILITY

❑ Your ability to deal with fluid complexity is a comfort to people who need a definitive agenda or plan. When you can keep the confusion as far away from them as possible and sort through myriad information to tell them what they need to know and do, they will feel safer and far more certain that all will be well.

❑ Sometimes the best laid plans spiral into chaos. By addressing problems before others even know any disruption happened, you help them remain in their comfort zone. Running a tight ship may not be so important to you, but running a steady one is. Many people need that kind of leadership to feel secure, and you provide it.

CREATE HOPE

❑ Not only can you help people get involved in activities that are right for them, you can also help them figure out what they shouldn't be doing and encourage them to stop doing it. They may feel trapped by calendars and commitments; you can free them. Inspire them to think about how to rearrange their responsibilities to make their lives more satisfying and productive.

❑ Before people can reorganize their time and responsibilities for a more fulfilling future, they may need a clear and concrete view of their current situation. Encourage them to fill out a calendar that shows everything they do in a week. Have them account for every hour. Then help them see ways to combine, eliminate, or add activities to enhance their quality of life.

LEADING *OTHERS* WITH STRONG ARRANGER

❑ This person will thrive when given a new challenge, so give him as much as you are able to, according to his knowledge and skill levels.

❑ This person may well have the talent to be a manager or supervisor. His Arranger talents enable him to figure out how people with very different strengths can work together.

❑ Pay attention to this person's other top themes. If he also has strong Discipline talents, he may be an excellent organizer, establishing routines and systems for getting things done.

❑ Understand that this person's modus operandi for team building is through trust and relationship. He may well reject someone who he believes is dishonest or does shoddy work.

LEADING WITH BELIEF

> People strong in the Belief theme have certain core values that are unchanging. Out of these values emerges a defined purpose for their life.

BUILD TRUST

- ❏ Ethical behavior is the foundation of respect and trust. Integrity is an expectation. To ensure fairness and promote unity, clearly communicate to others the behaviors you will and will not tolerate. Clarity on the front end can prevent misunderstandings and damage to relationships.

- ❏ The talent of Belief is more about an attitude of service than it is about a certain set of moral or spiritual beliefs. Show others what it means to be a servant leader. Get a team involved in doing something outside of themselves — something they do for the sole reason of helping another person or group. Demonstrate your Belief talents in actions that speak far louder than your words ever can. That level of integrity will earn you true respect.

SHOW COMPASSION

- ❏ Your values are a deep source of meaning for you. Talk with others about what's most meaningful in their lives. Just being a sounding board about something as important as core values builds relationships. Learn what's most important to the people in your life, whether you've known them a long time or just met them. Recognize that we all come from different backgrounds and go through various stages in our lives, and be accepting. Relationships can always grow. Listening creates a connection.

- ❏ Some bonds will be almost instantaneous. Common values will bring you close to some people quite rapidly — and sometimes for life. This can be a source of great joy in your life and theirs. Explore beliefs together, ask questions, and have conversations about what matters most in your lives. In these situations, relationships can grow surprisingly fast and remarkably deep.

❑ Take care not to create an "in" and an "out" crowd based on belief systems. Though you can never be "values neutral," nor should you be, you should consider the messages you send with the judgments you make.

PROVIDE STABILITY

❑ Some of your beliefs are etched in stone. Even in this ever-changing world, they never sway. This firm foundation can be a cornerstone of relationships, activities, and the work environment you create. Whether or not people believe as you do, they know where you stand and can be confident of the stability of those beliefs.

❑ Your passion equips you to fight. In these battles, strive to be seen as a leader who is fighting for something rather than one who is fighting against something. Being seen in a more positive light may help you enlist, engage, and retain more support for your cause. People will trust that you will fight for what's right. They take confidence in the strength of your convictions.

CREATE HOPE

❑ The meaning and purpose of your work will often provide direction for others, so talk about it; share its importance in your life. Remind people why their work is important and how it makes a difference in their lives and in the lives of others. Learn more about how they can live their talents and values through their work, and support them in finding those connections.

❑ Others may be less sure of their values than you are. If they are searching, ask them to take account of where they spend their time and money. The actual use of our time, talent, and treasure speaks volumes about what we really value.

LEADING *OTHERS* WITH STRONG BELIEF

❑ This person will have some powerful bedrock values. Figure out how to align her values with those of the organization. For example, talk with her about how your products and services make people's lives better, or discuss how your company embodies integrity and trust, or give her opportunities to go above and beyond to help colleagues and customers. This way, through her actions and words, she will make visible the values of your organization's culture.

❑ Realize that this person may place greater value on opportunities to provide higher levels of service than on opportunities to make more money. Find ways to enhance this natural service orientation, and you will see her at her best.

LEADING WITH COMMAND

> People strong in the Command theme have presence. They can take control of a situation and make decisions.

BUILD TRUST

❑ Because you're known for saying what you think, others trust that you won't play games. They can take what you say at face value, and they can be confident that you won't change your stripes once they've left the room. This directness builds trust, and trust builds relationships.

❑ Examine the correlations between your stated values and your actions. Are they consistent? Do they demonstrate integrity? Jot down the values that are most important to you. Can you think of recent examples of actions you have taken that confirm the integrity of your beliefs? Make this "walk the talk" checklist a regular part of your self-assessment, and ensure that others should trust what you say and respect your actions.

SHOW COMPASSION

❑ You feel things intensely and are capable of expressing great emotion. Do what you do naturally. Tell people how you feel and why they are important to you. Express the connection that others may be too reserved to say out loud. Your saying it first may free them to acknowledge that the feeling is mutual. And even if they are not there yet, you can launch the opportunity for a meaningful relationship. An expression of genuine caring, affection, or regard can be a powerful step toward initiating or deepening a bond between a leader and a follower.

❑ You use strong words. Express your sentiments to form a bond with others who will value what you stand for as a human being. Significant relationships are often formed on the basis of shared values, so stating your beliefs or passions can be a way for others to "find" you as a potential friend and champion. Invite others to join you based on your strong feelings and passionate beliefs — they may need the nudge.

☐ Sometimes others see the tough exterior of an individual with high Command and assume it's an impenetrable shell that protects him or her from all hurt. They may feel vulnerable and see you as invulnerable. Yet relationships depend on mutual vulnerability. Be open. Share your own pain and struggles. Letting others see the soft underbelly gives them equal power in the relationship and demonstrates trust.

PROVIDE STABILITY

☐ People know where you stand. The security of understanding that your convictions are not built on sinking sand allows people to feel confident that you will always be there for them and always stick to what you believe.

☐ Others come to you when they need someone to be strong for them — perhaps to shore up their own flagging courage or to step in and be a spokesperson for their needs. When their courage falters, they seek to "borrow" yours. Be aware of this need you fulfill, and ask others if they would like you to intervene on their behalf or accompany them on a difficult mission. Your "take charge" attitude steadies and reassures others in times of crisis. When faced with a particularly trying challenge, use your Command talents to assuage others' fears and convince them you have things under control.

CREATE HOPE

☐ Because you call it like you see it, others seek you out when they feel they can handle the truth. They might turn to others for support, but they go to you for an honest assessment of what they can and can't do, or should and shouldn't do. You don't shy away from offering advice. Ask them how committed they are to their current plan. Ask if they want your honest opinion. If they say yes, give it gently, but truthfully.

❑ Your powerful words inspire. Talk about the "why" of each mission without fearing to appear corny or sentimental. Your emotion allows others to rise to the occasion and give of themselves. They may be counting on you to give voice to the emotions that surround the cause. Paint an inspiring picture with your words.

LEADING *OTHERS* WITH STRONG COMMAND

❑ As much as you can, give this person room to lead and make decisions. He will not like to be supervised closely.

❑ When confronting this person, take firm action. And if necessary, require immediate restitution. Then arrange for him to be productive as soon as possible. He will get over his mistake quickly, and so should you.

❑ This person may intimidate others with his upfront, assertive style. You may need to consider whether or not his contribution justifies the occasional ruffled feathers. Rather than pushing him to learn how to be empathetic and polite, you'd make better use of your time by helping his colleagues understand that his assertiveness is part of what makes him effective — as long as he remains assertive rather than aggressive or offensive.

LEADING WITH COMMUNICATION

> People strong in the Communication theme generally find it easy to put their thoughts into words. They are good conversationalists and presenters.

BUILD TRUST

- ❏ You are able to use language to "spin" and to manipulate. But this is wearying over time. Remember that while spin can be persuasive in the short term, it exacts an emotional price. Make sure that you are not only effective, but ethical.

- ❏ Mutual respect is yours to build. Help people appreciate each other. Spend time "advertising" what they truly do well and what they are capable of contributing. Bear in mind that genuine praise encourages people, but false praise undermines them and is not taken seriously.

- ❏ Speak the same way about people to their faces as you do when they are not around. The consistency and honor of your words convey your integrity and shape the trust you build.

SHOW COMPASSION

- ❏ You have the power to capture people's emotions and put words to what they feel — sometimes words they cannot find themselves. This naturally draws others to you. So ask questions. Try to pinpoint the key issues people are trying to communicate, what joys or struggles they want to convey. Then give voice to those feelings. Helping people find the words to describe feelings is a powerful way to get them to express and process their own emotions, and it can support them on the way to making a plan of action.

- ❏ Language is a clue to culture. In any group, from a family to a corporation, think about what the words you use suggest. Names convey expectations. Do you tag your weekly meetings "department meetings," "staff meetings," "team meetings," "quality meetings"? Are they held in a "meeting room," a "conference room," a "break room," a "training center," or a "learning center"? Do you frame questions positively to help others see how much you care?

PROVIDE STABILITY

- ☐ Capture the successes of others in words, and relate those words back to them, preferably in writing. Use your talent for finding just the right words to praise, give feedback, and reassure. Your positive support of others' achievements will help them feel secure in their roles.

- ☐ Think about how you express time. Are we here for the long haul? Are we seeking immediate results or building a long-term reputation? Give people the sense that the big picture is what matters, and they will be free to experiment a little — even fail a little — to make things better for the future. As you choose your words, consider that stability is confidence in the long-term picture.

- ☐ Besides being the spokesperson, become the collector of your group's success stories. Create a brand for your group based on accumulated triumphs. This solid foundation will bolster your group's confidence for the future.

CREATE HOPE

- ☐ In an organizational setting, offer to be the person who composes any "wrap-up" communication. After meetings, send a summary e-mail. Capture the key points, and outline the actions people must take. Summarize successes. Express kudos to those who have done good work. You can encourage and inspire positive activities and outcomes as well as future accomplishments.

- ☐ Your words influence the impressions and expectations that people form about individuals and groups. Are you enhancing or undermining their image? When you speak to or about others, consciously choose words that offer encouragement, inspiration, and optimism.

☐ What terms and expressions do you use to paint pictures of the future? Your words can guide others. Consider the direction your words take people, and select them well. Those words may continue to inspire people longer than you imagine.

LEADING *OTHERS* WITH STRONG COMMUNICATION

☐ Ask this person to learn the folklore — the stories of interesting events in your organization. Then give her the opportunity to tell these stories to her colleagues. She will help bring your culture to life and thereby strengthen it.

☐ Ask this person to help some of the specialists in your organization make more engaging presentations. In some situations, you could ask her to volunteer to make the presentation for the specialist.

☐ If you send this person to public-speaking training, make sure to place her in a small class with advanced students and a top-level trainer. She will be irritated if she's in training with beginners.

LEADING WITH COMPETITION

> People strong in the Competition theme measure their progress against the performance of others. They strive to win first place and revel in contests.

BUILD TRUST

- ❑ Cheaters never prosper. Remember that winning at all costs isn't winning; it's defeating yourself. The price of winning can be greater than the pain of losing, so make sure your integrity remains intact when you push for that ultimate victory.

- ❑ Protect the trust that you have created with others. Sometimes you may need to "walk off the court" to keep your competitive emotions from damaging the respect you seek from others. Do it. Give yourself the release of an emotional reaction, but make sure you do it where the "judges" won't see you.

SHOW COMPASSION

- ❑ Competitors recognize one another almost immediately. When you find someone who shares your desire to win, you might choose to compete and push each other, or you might combine forces to create a championship team. Either way, it's an opportunity to form a bond based on a shared outlook.

- ❑ Can you engage others in a weekly competitive activity they enjoy? This is a way to create a lasting connection based on mutual interests and a shared approach to life's challenges. Engage the competitor, and build on that relationship opportunity.

- ❑ Competition, despite all the effort it produces, can leave a bad taste in the mouths of many. Try to bring out the fun side of competition; help it create emotional bonds rather than barriers. Remember that not everyone assigns the same emotional intensity to every activity they undertake, and remember to show that you accept and respect that they may have different reasons for being in the "game."

PROVIDE STABILITY

☐ A winning team promotes confidence. How can you help individuals or a team be their best? Position players so that they're building on their strengths; this gives them the best possible chance for success and security. Show people their capacity for peak performance based on their natural abilities.

☐ If you're in a losing battle now, remember your ultimate goal. Keep in mind that you're in it for the long haul, and help others see that too. Give them the peace of mind that this is an ongoing effort rather than a failure.

CREATE HOPE

☐ Champion others. Verbalize your belief that they can be the best at something. You may see potential in them that they cannot see. Point out the talents you notice in them, and help them learn how to turn those talents into strengths.

☐ What are the measures to beat in your organization? Put them out there so everyone has a clear target.

☐ Number one is the only position that counts in your book, so you tend to confine yourself to areas where you know you can win. As a leader, identify the market niches in which your group truly excels, and define its strengths and competitive edge in specific terms. In doing so, you set the group and the organization up for unparalleled success, which naturally increases your group's optimism.

☐ You are naturally attuned to real-world measures that assess achievements. Use this talent to identify world-class performance within and outside your organization and to identify industry benchmarks that truly count. Evaluate your organization against these standards, and inspire others to exceed them.

LEADING *OTHERS* WITH STRONG COMPETITION

❑ Measure this person's accomplishments against other people's — particularly other competitive people. You may decide to post the performance records of all your staff, but remember that only your competitive people will get a charge out of public comparison. Others may resent it or be mortified by the comparison.

❑ Set up contests for this person. Pit him against other competitors even if you have to find them in business units other than your own. Highly charged competitors want to compete with others who are very close to their skill level; matching them against modest achievers won't motivate them. Consider that one of the best ways to manage this person is to hire another competitive person who produces more.

❑ Talk about talents with this person. Like all competitors, he knows that it takes talent to be a winner. Name his talents. Tell him that he needs to marshal his talents to win. Do not "Peter Principle" this person by suggesting that winning means getting promoted.

LEADING WITH CONNECTEDNESS

> People strong in the Connectedness theme have faith in the links between all things. They believe there are few coincidences and that almost every event has a reason.

BUILD TRUST

☐ Your philosophy of life compels you to move beyond your own self-interests. Give voice to your beliefs. Take action on your values. When you move beyond self and give of what you have, others see the respect you have for every other human being, despite your differences. Respect is a natural byproduct of selfless acts.

☐ Seek out global or cross-cultural responsibilities that capitalize on your understanding of the commonalities inherent in humanity. Build global capability, and change the mindset of those who think in terms of "us" and "them." Behaving in the best interests of all parties is a sign of good faith and trustworthiness.

SHOW COMPASSION

☐ You seek the mutual bond. Develop good questions to ask so that you can quickly find common ground between you and each person you meet. Keep asking these questions until you find the interests you share. Affirm and celebrate the connections you find, and start there to build a foundation for a relationship.

☐ Once you have discovered areas of commonality with someone, show that you care by remembering to inquire about the belief or activity you share with her. Use this as a point of entry into deeper conversations about other parts of her life. Get to know her as a whole person, rather than limiting your connection to only one aspect of who she is.

❑ Your ability to bring people together around shared dreams and meanings is significant. You see the common thread in the greater whole. Take an active role in linking the lives of disparate individuals based on the connections you discover. Make others aware of the bonds they don't even know exist, and pave the road for friendship by helping strangers recognize the commonalities they have. You can help others make connections that influence the rest of their lives.

PROVIDE STABILITY

❑ Your sense of the bigger picture can bring calm in chaos. Point out the greater meaning you find in the events around you. Show others that a bump in the road is but a small part of a greater whole. Help them see the difference between what is constant in life and what is transitory. Put current difficulties in perspective.

❑ People feel safe when they are surrounded by what is comfortably familiar. When others need that sense of security, you can remind them of what is constant, what is shared. Help people remember that a network surrounds them. Simply knowing that they are not alone during difficult times can bring peace and confidence.

❑ Faith can be a foundational strength when it is shared. If faith is part of your relationship with another person, your support may be very important in times of uncertainty or fear. Reach out when you know someone needs the assurance that shared faith can provide.

CREATE HOPE

❑ It may surprise you when others are slow to discover the connections that you so easily see. Help them understand the interrelatedness you find in events and people. Broaden their worldview by helping them see a bigger picture. How could they take their own talent to a new level by applying it somewhere they've never thought to apply it? How might they partner with someone they see as much different from themselves? Get them thinking in new ways by sharing your broader vision.

❑ You are aware of the boundaries and borders created by organizational structure, but you treat them as seamless and fluid. Use your Connectedness talents to break down silos that prevent shared knowledge across industry, functional, and hierarchical divisions within or between organizations. Encourage different groups to work together for their shared goals.

❑ Help people see the links among their talents, their actions, their mission, and the success of the larger group or organization. When people believe in what they are doing and feel like they are part of something bigger, commitment to achievement is enhanced.

LEADING *OTHERS* WITH STRONG CONNECTEDNESS

❑ This person is likely to have a spiritual orientation and perhaps a strong faith. Your knowledge and, at the very least, acceptance of her spirituality will enable her to become increasingly comfortable around you.

❑ This person may be receptive to thinking about and developing the mission for your organization. She naturally feels like she is part of something larger than herself, and she will enjoy contributing to the impact of an overall statement or goal.

LEADING WITH CONSISTENCY

> People strong in the Consistency theme are keenly aware of the need to treat people the same. They try to treat everyone in the world with consistency by setting up clear rules and adhering to them.

BUILD TRUST

❑ Cultivate trust by subjecting yourself to whatever rules or programs you approve for your group or organization. When you live by the rules, it demonstrates your respect for principle, sets the tone for equality, and encourages peaceful compliance.

❑ Though others may take advantage of the perks of their position, your egalitarian mindset likely rejects them and prefers to live by the same set of expectations and standards as the larger population in your organization. Fully adapt this "equal footing" policy to win respect and solidify your constituency.

SHOW COMPASSION

❑ Being able to predict how another person will act — and react — helps us confidently plot the course for a relationship. Think about how Consistency influences the relationships others are able to build with you. Are you always there in times of need? Do you consistently show compassion and caring? Analyze the foundations of your closest relationships, and see what you discover about the role your Consistency talents play. Then consider how you can use this pattern to expand the number of friendships in your life.

❑ When you show your appreciation for the value another person places on fairness and equity, you validate who he or she is and form the foundation of support and understanding. You may fare best in relationships with others who live their lives according to similar principles. Seek out opportunities to commend those whose values and ideals you admire. Tell them how they make the world a better place. By doing so, you show them that you notice what they do best and that you care about them.

PROVIDE STABILITY

❑ Others find comfort in knowing what is expected and what is not tolerated. Let people know the norms so that they do not unintentionally violate them.

❑ When others know your codes of behavior, they can count on you to be constant in your application of them. Verbalize the importance of consistency in your expectations of yourself and others. By doing this, people will not only know the rules, but also their underlying principles. This will help them predict your behavior in situations the rules don't cover.

CREATE HOPE

❑ When others come to you for help, it may be that they're seeking the comfort of your consistency. Your assurance that they can count on you to be there for them will be encouraging.

❑ You might find that you are a champion of the underdog. This should feel good to you — it means that your support is not destined only for those in the lead, but for all. Encourage those who struggle. Be sure to take into account their personal pattern of success. Perhaps they are striving to achieve in a way that does not suit them well and they need some redirection. Help them make the most of their opportunities by finding a pattern that works for them.

LEADING *OTHERS* WITH STRONG CONSISTENCY

❑ When you need to put consistent practices in place for your organization, ask this person to help establish routines.

❑ When this person is in an analytical role, ask her to work on group, rather than individual, data. She is likely to be more adept at discovering generalizations that can be made about the group rather than particulars about a certain individual.

❑ If, as a manager, you struggle with situations in which rules must be applied equally, absolutely, and with no favoritism, ask this person to help you deal with them. The explanations and justifications will come naturally to her.

❑ In situations in which it is necessary to treat diverse people equally, ask this person to contribute to the development of the rules and procedures.

LEADING WITH CONTEXT

> People strong in the Context theme enjoy thinking about the past. They understand the present by researching its history.

BUILD TRUST

- ❏ Relate stories of your own life that you think will resonate with others. Being vulnerable enough to share a bit of your own past can be a gateway to trust.

- ❏ Encourage mutual sharing of histories and life events if others are willing, and honor their trust when they confide in you.

SHOW COMPASSION

- ❏ You're interested in the roots, the history, and the formative moments in the lives of those around you. For you, a great conversation starter is "Tell me about a turning point in your life." Ask questions that elicit stories that will be as fun for you to hear as they are for others to tell. Showing your interest will demonstrate that you care.

- ❏ Remember the details of stories you've heard someone tell, and use them as ongoing connecting points with that person. Looking across a room and making eye contact when something you've heard holds meaning for the two of you shows that you listened, remembered, and connected to the individual.

PROVIDE STABILITY

- ❏ Stability is certainly linked to Context. The sense that nothing in the universe is new means that we have experienced these things before and will do so again. Having survived previous trials indicates our fortitude and resilience and gives us the confidence and courage to find new ways to triumph.

❑ History teaches patience, and putting things in perspective encourages understanding and security. Articulate the historical perspective on the issues people face today. Help them see the past as a teacher, and find wisdom in its lessons.

CREATE HOPE

❑ Ask others questions like "How did you come to that decision?" and "Have you ever dealt with an issue or situation like this in the past?" Your good questions and gentle guidance can help others get perspective on a situation and help them avoid recurring errors. You can give people hope by helping them recognize the strength they have already demonstrated — and will demonstrate again.

❑ Help people make sense of their lives and circumstances by showing them how to link their own history with their present and future. Work with them to develop a timeline of their lives that includes significant decisions, trials, triumphs, and turning points. Ask them what they learned at each juncture. And help them consider what they can do now as a result of what they've learned.

❑ Boiling down complex ideas or proposals to their most basic elements helps you understand the original purpose or reasoning behind them. Trace the evolution of a plan or idea back to its inception, and clarify the purpose of its direction to those who may question it. You will strengthen the mission of your team.

❑ Remind your colleagues that the values and goals of your organization are based on wisdom derived from the past. Keep the history of your enterprise alive by retelling stories that capture its essence. These stories can offer guidance and inspiration in the present through understanding the insights of the past. Can you be the keeper of the wisdom — or at least initiate the collection and recording of the wisdom? Future generations will thank you.

LEADING *OTHERS* WITH STRONG CONTEXT

❑ When you ask this person to do something, take time to explain the thinking that led to the request. He needs to understand the background of a course of action before he can commit to it.

❑ No matter what the subject matter, ask this person to collect revealing stories, highlight the key discovery from each one, and perhaps build a class around them.

❑ Ask this person to collect anecdotes of people behaving in a way that exemplifies the cornerstones of your organization's culture. His stories, retold in newsletters, training classes, websites, videos, and so on, will strengthen your culture.

LEADING WITH DELIBERATIVE

People strong in the Deliberative theme are best described by the serious care they take in making decisions or choices. They anticipate the obstacles.

BUILD TRUST

❑ You inspire trust because you are cautious and considerate regarding sensitive topics. Use these talents by taking on opportunities to handle delicate issues and conflicts.

❑ Others respect the time you dedicate to doing things right and to doing the right things. Let them know when you need time to think before making a decision. Trust them to appreciate that you have their best interests in mind.

SHOW COMPASSION

❑ You understand the importance and weight of each relationship, and you take this responsibility seriously. Once you've chosen to add someone to your life, tend the relationship well. Invest in activities and conversations that keep you close, and reveal your heart to the people who matter most. Lifetime relationships are hard to find, as you know, and they deserve and require your attention and love.

❑ Understand that your praise is rare — and precious to many. So when you commend others, consider marking the occasion with a tangible reminder of your recognition. Giving them a visible token of your appreciation will help the memory of your rare praise last for a long time.

PROVIDE STABILITY

❑ Rather than take foolhardy risks, you are apt to approach a decision cautiously. Trust your instincts when you believe something is "too good to be true." Your deliberation and caution make others feel protected and secure about the conclusions you reach.

- ❏ Others will appreciate the careful thought that goes into each decision you make. Tell them about the options that you have analyzed and why you have chosen a particular course. Consider that they have a stake in the decision too. Ask for and weigh their input as carefully as you do your own.

CREATE HOPE

- ❏ Temper the tendency of others to move haphazardly into action by declaring a "consideration" period before decisions are made. Your caution can serve to steer others away from folly and toward wise choices.

- ❏ When you know a great deal about a topic, offer others the benefits of the research and analysis you have done. Encourage them to try something if you believe it's the right thing for them to do. Show them the supporting evidence.

LEADING *OTHERS* WITH STRONG DELIBERATIVE

- ❏ Do not position this person in a role that requires snap judgments. She is likely to feel uncomfortable making decisions on gut instinct alone.

- ❏ When caution is required, such as circumstances that are sensitive to legal, safety, or accuracy issues, ask this person to take the lead. She will instinctively anticipate where the dangers might lie and how to keep you protected.

- ❏ This person is likely to excel at negotiating contracts, especially behind the scenes. As far as you can within the confines of her job description, ask her to play this role.

- ❏ Do not ask this person to be a greeter, rainmaker, or networker for your organization. The kind of effusiveness that these roles require may not be in her repertoire.

- ❏ In her relationships, this person will be selective and discriminating. Consequently, do not move her quickly from team to team. She needs to feel assured that the people she surrounds herself with are competent and trustworthy, and this confidence takes time to build.

❏ This person will be known as someone who gives praise sparingly, but when she does, it is truly deserved.

LEADING WITH DEVELOPER

People strong in the Developer theme recognize and cultivate the potential in others. They spot the signs of each small improvement and derive satisfaction from these improvements.

BUILD TRUST

❑ Doing something good for the sake of another is a sign of character and an invitation to trust. Extend yourself to others by helping them see their own potential and offering to work with them to develop it. This will increase the breadth and depth of your relationships, and you will enjoy watching them grow.

❑ Try not to be hurt when others look for an ulterior motive in your good deeds. It may take them time to trust you when you show interest in their personal development. Allow them to see you in action for weeks, months, or even years before expecting their full confidence. They may not trust as easily as you do.

SHOW COMPASSION

❑ You take genuine delight in people's growth and development. Your natural talent for focusing on others is a gift to those you nurture. Cheer for them, and let them know that you believe in them. Your compassionate caring touches their hearts and places you squarely on their side. They will never forget the support you offer so easily.

❑ "We learn best from those we love" is a quote you understand and appreciate. Who loves you? Whom do you love? Be sure to get close enough to not only teach and guide, but to love. Communicate your feelings. Your impact will last forever.

PROVIDE STABILITY

- ❑ As you begin working with another person on her development, first acknowledge the progress you've already seen. This provides a basis of confidence and security. You can make taking the next step less intimidating by reassuring her that you are confident she can do it because of what she's already proven herself able to do. Express your certainty that the next goal is within her reach.

- ❑ Developers help others step over comfort thresholds. You provide a "safe zone" where people have permission to strive and fail and strive again. Set others up for success by letting them know that more than one attempt is likely to be necessary before ultimate success results. Helping people set the right expectations provides security that produces the confidence to try again.

- ❑ Encourage people to dig deep into their talents and to put them to the test. With you, they have a cushion for failure and will not feel the full force of it. You provide support so that they can take the risks necessary to make the most of their talents.

CREATE HOPE

- ❑ Challenge others by asking good questions that stretch their imagination. What's the most they've ever done? How much do they imagine they could do? What do they dream of doing? What would they do if there were no obstacles, no barriers to their choices?

- ❑ Your growth-nurturing approach is your spontaneous response to those around you and makes you an inspirational mentor to many. Consider the moves your best mentors made, and take a lesson from them. Adopt the ones that are right for you, and use them to encourage and champion those you are mentoring.

❑ You will be compelled to counsel more people than you possibly can. To fulfill this inner drive, consider being a "mentor for the moment." Many of the most poignant and memorable developmental moments occur in a mere instant when the right words are delivered at the right time — words that clarify understanding, re-ignite a passion, open eyes to an opportunity, and change a life course. Look for opportunities to magnify moments.

LEADING *OTHERS* WITH STRONG DEVELOPER

❑ Position this person so that he can help others in the organization grow. For example, give him the opportunity to mentor one or two people or to teach a class on a company topic, such as safety, benefits, or customer service. If necessary, pay the fee for him to belong to a local training organization.

❑ This person might be a good candidate for a supervisor, team leader, or manager role. If he is already a manager or executive, look to his business unit for people who can be transferred to positions with greater responsibilities in the organization. He develops people and prepares them for the future.

❑ Be aware that this person may protect struggling performers long past the time when they should have been moved or terminated. Help him focus his developing instincts on setting people up to achieve success and not on supporting people who are enduring hardship. The best developmental action he can take with these people is to find them a different opportunity where they can truly excel.

LEADING WITH DISCIPLINE

People strong in the Discipline theme enjoy routine and structure.
Their world is best described by the order they create.

BUILD TRUST

❑ You never let yourself off the hook, and others will respect
you for your uncompromising standards. Hold yourself to
the standards you set, and your actions will reflect your
integrity.

❑ Others can count on you to make sure every detail is
executed exactly right. Discipline can become the basis for
trust when people see that their expectations are met time
and time again. They will learn to respect your consistent
delivery.

SHOW COMPASSION

❑ Your powerful sense of order can make you a tremendous
partner to those who rely on your discipline to supplement
their own. Find and celebrate the positive traits others
possess that you do not, and build a relationship based on
mutual appreciation. Someone learns to rely on you, and you
on them, when a complementary partnership is at its best.

❑ You can show others kindness by attending to the details
that they are sure to miss. Adopt the mindset of a caring
friend, and seek ways to free others from the details that
bog them down. You can make their lives better — and win
appreciation at the same time.

PROVIDE STABILITY

❑ You are predictable and consistent. You do what is required
when it is required — if not before. Share your timelines with
others, and let them see the consistent progress you make as

promised. People will feel safe entrusting you with projects when they see that your actions always follow your words.

❑ Not everyone is blessed with your sense of order. Share with others the calmness and composure you get from order by letting them know that you have situations under control. Help them see that each part will be accomplished in its time, and the entire project will follow according to plan. Others will be freed to do what they do well when they know that nothing important can slip through the cracks.

CREATE HOPE

❑ Your performance objectives spur your efforts; you like to get things done each day and each week. Noticing your productivity, others may take their cue from your performance objectives as well. Detail your tasks, goals, and timelines, and share them with interested teammates who may use your example to inspire their own work efforts.

❑ Trying to impose your systems and structures on others who lack strong Discipline talents simply won't work. Rather than trying to "convert" those who appear to need your sense of order, seek to discover what they do well; then support and encourage them in those areas.

LEADING *OTHERS* WITH STRONG DISCIPLINE

❑ Give this person the opportunity to bring structure to a haphazard or chaotic situation. Because she will not be comfortable in such shapeless, messy circumstances — and don't expect her to be — she will not rest until order and predictability are restored.

❑ When there are many things that need to get done in a set time period, remember this person's need to prioritize. Take the time to set priorities together, and once the schedule is set, stick to it.

❑ If appropriate, ask this person to help you plan and organize your own work. You might enlist her to review your time management system or even your proposal for reengineering some of your department's processes. Tell her colleagues that this is one of her talents, and encourage them to ask her for similar help.

❑ This person excels at developing routines that help her work efficiently. If she is forced to work in a situation that requires flexibility and responsiveness, encourage her to devise a set number of routines, each appropriate for a certain set of circumstances. This way, she will have a predictable response to fall back on, no matter what the surprise.

LEADING WITH EMPATHY

> People strong in the Empathy theme can sense the feelings of other people by imagining themselves in others' lives or situations.

BUILD TRUST

☐ Help others articulate and frame complex emotions when they're faced with a worrisome situation. Respect their feelings, and allow them the freedom to express what they need to express, whether or not your feelings mirror theirs. Acknowledge and deal with these emotions honestly to build trust.

☐ Because trust is paramount to you, many of your associates are likely to feel comfortable approaching you to share thoughts, feelings, concerns, and needs. Your discretion and desire to be genuinely helpful will be greatly valued.

SHOW COMPASSION

☐ Witnessing the happiness of others brings you pleasure. Consequently, you are likely to be attuned to opportunities to highlight people's successes and positively reinforce their achievements. At each opportunity, deliver a kind word of appreciation or recognition. By doing so, you are likely to make a profound and engaging impression on that person.

☐ Sometimes you have the ability to understand what others are feeling before they've recognized it themselves. This uncanny awareness can be unnerving or comforting, depending on how it's shared. Ask questions to gently guide people toward recognition of what you already suspect. Help them name their feelings and create their own path to self-discovery, and you will be a valued partner.

PROVIDE STABILITY

❏ Sensitive to the feelings of others, you readily gauge the emotional tone of a room. Use your talents to forge a bridge of understanding and mutual support. Your Empathy talents will be especially important during trying times because they will demonstrate your concern as a leader, thereby building security and loyalty.

❏ Patience and understanding are your hallmarks. Take time to hear people out; don't rush to judgment. Giving people time and space to sort out their own thoughts and feelings in a safe environment promotes their sense of stability and tranquility.

CREATE HOPE

❏ Others are likely to choose you as a confidante or mentor. Affirm that this is a satisfying relationship for you so they feel welcome to approach you. Encourage them by putting words to what you sense about their aspirations; inspire and guide their dreams by imagining with them.

❏ Your Empathy talents allow you to anticipate events and reactions. Because you are observant of how others are feeling, you are likely to intuit what is about to happen in the organization before it becomes common knowledge. Help people to be aware as positive emotions build, so as a group, you can capitalize on this to create hope.

LEADING *OTHERS* WITH STRONG EMPATHY

❏ Pay attention, but don't overreact if this person cries. Tears are part of his life. He may sense the joy or tragedy in another person's life more poignantly than even that person does.

❏ Help this person see his Empathy talent as a special gift. It may come so naturally to him that he thinks everyone feels what he feels, or he may be embarrassed by his strength of feeling. Show him how to use his talents to everyone's advantage.

❑ Test this person's ability to make decisions instinctively rather than logically. He may not be able to articulate why he thinks a certain action is right, but he will often be right nonetheless. Ask him "What is your gut feeling about what we should do?"

❑ Arrange for this person to work with positive, optimistic people. He will pick up on their feelings and be motivated. Conversely, steer him away from pessimists and cynics. They will depress him.

LEADING WITH FOCUS

> People strong in the Focus theme can take a direction, follow through, and make the corrections necessary to stay on track. They prioritize, then act.

BUILD TRUST

❑ Others will respect you because you know what's important, and you keep your attention there. Make sure that you're not delegating non-essentials. Before you ask someone to do something, ask yourself if it affects ultimate performance. If it's not worth your time, perhaps it's not worth anyone's time, and you don't even have to ask. Others will trust your judgment.

❑ As a person with strong Focus talents, you know that life is about choices. Remember that everyone is responsible for their own decisions. Demonstrate to others that you understand and respect their choices in life.

SHOW COMPASSION

❑ Take a step back and think broadly about the priorities in your life. Use your Focus talents to target not only the projects that are important, but also the people. Set goals and strategies for giving those people the time and attention they deserve as partners in your life. Include these goals on your daily to-do lists, and check off what you accomplish.

❑ In whom should you be investing at work? Who makes your life better every day through their efforts on the job? Show appreciation to those who enable you to be so efficient. Acknowledge their role in your effectiveness, and don't forget to reach out when they need your help too.

PROVIDE STABILITY

☐ Expand the effects of your Focus talents by extending the period of time you usually plan in advance. For example, if you typically plan one year ahead, try planning three years out. Gradually increase the length of time you encompass in your forecasting. Share your thoughts with others. Knowing that you are focusing on and thinking about the long term will give them security now.

☐ When you share long-term goals with your family and your work teams, tell them that they are part of your future projections. Give them the assurance that they are valued and needed and will be there with you.

CREATE HOPE

☐ Over a lifetime, we accrue responsibilities and tasks that may have ceased to have meaning for us. Help others clear some of the accumulated clutter of their lives. Ask questions like "What are the most important priorities in your life and your work?" "What do you love about doing this?" and "What would happen if you stopped doing this?" By tackling these questions, you can help people focus — or refocus — their energies and offer them a fresh outlook on the future.

☐ Invest in your organization by guiding the career trajectories of your company's most promising protégés. When mentoring others, you can assist them in crafting well-defined career paths and action plans to secure their major aspirations.

☐ Having measurable, specific, and tangible performance objectives is critical to your effectiveness. You relish setting regular "mini goals" for yourself because they keep your Focus talents sharp. Share your goals, measurement systems, and performance objectives with associates. In doing so, you will increase the sense of "team" and inspire them to track their personal progress in relation to the larger organizational objectives.

LEADING *OTHERS* WITH STRONG FOCUS

❑ Set goals with timelines, and then let this person figure out how to achieve them. He will work best in an environment where he can control his work events.

❑ Check in with this person on a regular basis — as often as he indicates would be helpful. He will thrive on this regular attention because he likes talking about goals and his progress toward them. Ask him how often you should meet to discuss goals and objectives.

❑ Don't expect this person to always be sensitive to the feelings of others; getting his work done often takes top priority. If he also has strong Empathy talents, this effect will obviously be lessened. Nonetheless, be aware of the possibility that he may trample on others' feelings as he marches toward his goal.

❑ This person does not thrive in constantly changing situations. To manage this, when describing the change to him, use language that he will be more receptive to. For example, talk about it in terms of "new goals" and "new measures of success," giving the change trajectory and purpose. This is the way he naturally thinks.

❑ Arrange for this person to attend a time management seminar. He may not naturally excel at this, but because his Focus theme pushes him to move toward his goals as fast as possible, he will appreciate the greater efficiency that effective time management brings.

LEADING WITH FUTURISTIC

> People strong in the Futuristic theme are inspired by the future and what could be. They inspire others with their visions of the future.

BUILD TRUST

❑ When helping others imagine what could be, make sure that your visions are grounded in reality. Many people do not find it as easy as you do to envision what things will look like decades later, so provide as much detail as you can about what they can do to be a part of the future. A realistic attitude will help build trust and confidence in your visionary ideas.

❑ Given your natural ability to look ahead, at times you may see disturbing trends on the horizon. Even if you enjoy talking about possibilities more than problems, you may be able to help people see and eliminate potential roadblocks before they cause any difficulties. Others will come to depend on you for this and trust what you see.

SHOW COMPASSION

❑ One of the best ways to make a connection with another human being is to listen. Ask the people you lead about their dreams. Have them describe their ideal future to you. Somewhere in their story, your Futuristic talents are likely to find a connection. Build on that connection by asking questions, helping them find more clarity as they put feelings to words. They will feel closer to you simply because you took an interest in their hopes and dreams for the future.

❑ You see the future more clearly than others. Do a little dreaming for people. Tell them that these dreams are possible if they set their sights on them. Perhaps you see talents in them that they are blind to, or opportunities they have not considered. Investing your time and energy in thinking about possibilities and what is good for other people shows caring and friendship. It shows you are a leader.

PROVIDE STABILITY

☐ People sometimes exaggerate the fear of the present because they cannot see beyond to a future when "this too shall pass." You have the gift of perspective; your thinking is not bound by present circumstances. Help others share the calm you possess, knowing that another day will come, and all this will be behind them.

☐ As you think about the future, be sure to "check in" with the people you lead about their emotions. If the visions you have are too distant for them to imagine, or if too much seems uncertain, they may get worried or uncomfortable. Ask people how they see themselves in the scenarios you discuss, and help them know that these are "what if" pictures, not "must be" plans. They are the ones in control of their destiny.

CREATE HOPE

☐ Because you have the gift of future thinking, it should come as no surprise that people choose you as their sounding board when they seek direction and guidance. You may have been playing the role of a guide for others your whole life. Think through this role. Consider what questions you should be asking. What do others need from you? How do you find out? Having a set of questions to ask when others seek you out may help you match your contribution to their expectations and aspirations.

☐ You inspire others with your images of the future. When you articulate your vision, be sure to describe the future in detail with vivid words and metaphors so that others can better comprehend your expansive thinking. Make your ideas and strategies more concrete via sketches, step-by-step action plans, or mock-up models so that your associates can readily grasp your intent.

LEADING *OTHERS* WITH STRONG FUTURISTIC

☐ Give this person time to think about, write about, and plan for the products and services your organization will need in the future. Create opportunities for her to share her perspective in company newsletters, meetings, or industry conventions.

☐ Put this person on the organization's planning committee. Have her present her data-based vision of what the organization might look like in three years. And have her repeat this presentation every six months or so. This way, she can refine it with new data and insights.

☐ When your organization needs people to embrace change, ask this person to put these changes in the context of the organization's future needs. Have her make a presentation or write an article that puts these new directions in perspective. She can help others rise above their present uncertainties and become almost as excited as she is about the possibilities of the future.

LEADING WITH HARMONY

People strong in the Harmony theme look for consensus. They don't enjoy conflict; rather, they seek areas of agreement.

BUILD TRUST

❑ You show others respect by valuing their input and helping them be heard. At times, you may need to point out that each person's point of view is valuable and deserves respect, if not agreement. Learn to briefly, yet effectively, communicate the value of listening.

❑ The loudest voices are not the only ones that should be heard. Sometimes you may need to stop the debate, open up the floor, and help each person have a say. When you do, make sure this environment is one of trust and respect so that those with quieter voices feel comfortable sharing their opinions. By making it clear that decisions are better when every voice is heard, others will have faith in your motives and be more likely to share discussion time equitably.

SHOW COMPASSION

❑ Your Harmony talents make life more pleasant. You reduce stress by reducing conflict and friction. Invest some time in conceptualizing the greater purpose of your organization. When tensions mount, remind others of the overriding mission that binds you all together. In addition to cooling the conflict, your actions help others rise to another level that is based on a shared purpose. Others will be drawn to you because you are considerate of everyone's opinions, and you honor their views.

❑ Seeking common ground comes naturally to you. Your quest for harmony between individuals and groups shows others that you care and enhances one-to-one and group relationships. How many points of commonality can you find per interaction? Count them, and see if you can increase your average over time. The greater the number of connecting points, the greater the opportunity for establishing significant and lasting relationships.

PROVIDE STABILITY

❑ You naturally provide peace and understanding. Your approach allows everyone to stay connected to the group, even when opinions differ. Remind others that the strength of a group is the ability to respectfully bring a variety of ideas to the table. Your knack for appeasing those with opposing views helps everyone in the group feel a sense of security that no matter what the issue, the group will remain intact.

❑ You calm others by smoothing the waters and helping everyone keep a level head. You ensure that no one is hurt by thoughtless words spoken in passion. Creating an atmosphere of dignity and respect helps others feel safe when it's their turn to share their views.

CREATE HOPE

❑ Establish and encourage interactions and forums in which people feel that their opinions are truly being heard. In doing so, you will promote engagement, raise individual achievement levels, and contribute to the overall performance of teams. This will, in turn, create hope for the future.

❑ Polish your talent for resolution without agitation by gathering skills and knowledge. Become skilled in moving through the steps of conflict resolution, and invite someone to learn with you. Encourage and inspire each other to become experts in finding solutions through consensus. Learn and teach at the same time.

LEADING *OTHERS* WITH STRONG HARMONY

❑ Find areas and issues on which you and this person agree, and regularly review these topics with him. Surround him with other people who are strong in Harmony. He will always be more focused, more productive, and more creative when he knows that he's supported.

❑ Don't be surprised if this person agrees with you even when you are wrong. Sometimes, for the sake of Harmony, he may nod his head despite judging your idea a poor one. Consequently, you may need other people who instinctively voice their opinions to help keep your thinking clear.

LEADING WITH IDEATION

People strong in the Ideation theme are fascinated by ideas. They are able to find connections between seemingly disparate phenomena.

BUILD TRUST

- ❑ The purpose behind your pursuit of what's new can help others trust you to make good choices. Explain the "why" behind what you do. Help people see that you are seeking to improve the status quo, to better explain the world, and to make discoveries that ultimately serve humanity.

- ❑ Make things simple. All your ideas, possibilities, and tangents can be confusing to some people. You see the simplicity of the underlying principles; articulate that to others so that they can see it too. The clearer things seem to people, the more certain they can be that you are doing what is right and makes sense. Help people make connections between what is and what can be.

SHOW COMPASSION

- ❑ Others have great appreciation for your creative imagination and your continual quest for new ideas. Invite them along for the ride. Ask them to dream with you. Shared excitement about ideas and possibilities, even from vastly different fields and approaches, can be a foundation for a mutually satisfying relationship.

- ❑ Partner with others who have a practical bent — people who can make your ideas realistic and bring them to fruition. You can be their inspiration; they can help you realize your dreams. Your differences are what bind you together and make each of you more successful than you would be on your own. Show consideration and appreciation for what others bring to the table.

PROVIDE STABILITY

☐ Stability and Ideation might seem at odds. You are always searching for ways to break from convention and look at things from a new angle. Verbalize the fact that you're not seeking to destroy what is — rather, you want to make things better. You understand that security doesn't come from maintaining the status quo and doing things the way they've always been done; security is about making sure you are prepared for the future.

☐ You must take risks. Still, you can calm others by educating them that those risks are calculated, not reckless. Give others confidence by helping them see the logic behind your pursuit of what's new, and keep them informed along the way.

CREATE HOPE

☐ You are a natural fit with people in research and development; you appreciate the mindset of the visionaries and dreamers in your organization. Spend time with imaginative staff members, and sit in on their brainstorming sessions. Invite people you know who have good ideas to join as well. As a leader with exceptional Ideation talents, you can contribute to inspirational ideas and make them happen.

☐ Find people in other walks of life who like to talk about ideas, and build mutually supportive and satisfying relationships. Their knowledge and dreams about an area that is foreign to you can inspire you. Feed one another's need for big thinking.

LEADING *OTHERS* WITH STRONG IDEATION

☐ This person has creative ideas. Be sure to position her where her ideas will be valued.

☐ Encourage this person to think of useful ideas or insights that can be shared with your best customers. From Gallup's research, it is clear that when a company deliberately teaches its customers something, their level of loyalty increases.

❑ This person needs to know that everything fits together. When decisions are made, take time to show her how each one is rooted in the same theory or concept.

❑ When a particular decision does not fit into an overarching concept, be sure to explain to this person that the decision is an exception or an experiment. Without this explanation, she may start to worry that the organization is becoming incoherent.

LEADING WITH INCLUDER

People strong in the Includer theme are accepting of others. They show awareness of those who feel left out and make an effort to include them.

BUILD TRUST

- ❑ Your utter lack of elitism inspires respect and honor. Others can rely on you to find common ground and recognize the contribution each person makes to the whole.

- ❑ Automatic acceptance is part of your wiring. You don't debate the merits and drawbacks of including someone. If someone is there, he should be welcomed and brought into the fold. Help others see past what's on the outside, and ask them to consider how others feel. Everyone will know that you are a person who deserves respect when they see the respect that you give to others.

SHOW COMPASSION

- ❑ Everyone needs an Includer as a friend. You help people feel welcome and immediately make them a part of something larger than themselves. You reach out and invite others to join when they are feeling like outsiders looking in. Never hesitate to invite, even when rebuffed. Know that you are always doing the right thing.

- ❑ Nurture the new folks in your organization. Be a first friend. Know their names, and introduce them to others, helping them find connecting points. You will collect many best friends this way. It's hard to forget the person who first made you feel like you belonged in a new place where you felt uncertain.

PROVIDE STABILITY

- ❏ Stability is fostered when everyone knows that they will not be excluded. Being consistent with your invitations and open to a wide variety of people helps others know that they too find a welcome whenever they need it. That's security.

- ❏ Your attitude that "there's always room for one more" will promote inclusion rather than competition when someone new joins the group. When others see that the circle expands to accommodate all, they will feel less territorial and more secure that they have a place in the fold. Make them feel even more confident by asking them to take on some of the orientation for new people.

CREATE HOPE

- ❏ Be an "Includer coach." Share your ideas for helping people feel welcome. Others may require a caring nudge to get them to step outside their comfort zone and make the first move to add someone to their inner circle. When you offer that nudge, you give two people a bit more opportunity for growth in the future.

- ❏ Consider that people will relate to each other through you. You are a conduit for information; you can connect with all of the people in a group and keep them effectively connected to each other. Watch as this network you have created multiplies by the day.

LEADING *OTHERS* WITH STRONG INCLUDER

- ❏ This person is interested in making everyone feel like part of the team. Ask him to work on an orientation program for new employees. He will be excited to think about ways to welcome new recruits.

- ❏ You can capitalize on this person's Includer talents by focusing them on your customers. Properly positioned, he may prove to be very effective at breaking any barriers between customer and company.

❑ Because this person probably will not appreciate elite products or services made for a select category of customer, position him to work on products or services that are designed for a broad market. He will enjoy planning ways to cast a wide net.

❑ In certain situations, it may be appropriate to ask this person to be your organization's link to community social agencies.

LEADING WITH INDIVIDUALIZATION

> People strong in the Individualization theme are intrigued with the unique qualities of each person. They have a gift for figuring out how people who are different can work together productively.

BUILD TRUST

- ❑ Sometimes you know more than people would like you to know. Keep strict confidences, and only share your insights with a person one-on-one. She should be the one to decide if she wants you to relate those insights to others.

- ❑ Others trust your instincts about people's unique qualities. Continue to build on that trust by focusing on the positive as much as you can when you are asked to share your impressions about someone.

- ❑ Stand behind your tendency to treat each person individually according to need, strength, and style. Many may see this as "playing favorites" and distrust you. Be prepared to defend your Individualization from a performance-excellence standpoint, as well as from a humane perspective. This will give others confidence in your decisions.

SHOW COMPASSION

- ❑ Others are often surprised at the depth of your insights about them, especially when you've known them only a short time. You've probably heard "How did you know that?" many times. As relationships develop, others will want to hear in greater depth your thoughts and insights regarding their actions, motivations, and talents. You are a mirror for them, and you offer a valuable perspective. Ask them to tell you more about themselves, and test your insights. Accept and affirm what they have to tell you.

❑ You may have the gift of gifting — choosing the perfect gift for another person — even someone you don't know particularly well. Finding a small token and giving it at an unexpected time can be a quick relationship builder. Give yourself permission to reach out in this way, and enjoy the rewarding looks of surprise and delight. Who can resist a perfectly chosen gift? Bring joy into others' lives with little surprises.

PROVIDE STABILITY

❑ Your awareness is essential to providing stability. By being attuned to others' desires and needs, you can help them because you can position them in the right place. Their confidence grows because they are being asked to do what they do best.

❑ "All generalizations are false, including this one" is a phrase you might enjoy. Knowing that you are conscious of each person's special circumstances helps him or her feel understood and secure. Let people know that despite the rules or the classic wisdom, you will take their unique talents and needs into account when making decisions about opportunities they can pursue.

CREATE HOPE

❑ Sometimes people are more predictable to you than they are to themselves. Use your talent to notice others' consistent behavior patterns to help them see things they can't. You might be able to help them capitalize on talents they seldom use intentionally or avoid pitfalls that repeatedly ensnare them. Kindly give them feedback to help them streamline their dreams and aspirations.

❑ You are instinctively aware that individuals will be most productive when their environments are suited to their talents. Wherever appropriate, implement organizational policies that allow your associates to work in their own style

— policies that allow people to express their individuality in the clothes they wear, how they decorate their offices, and the hours they work. Through these policies, you will engage and inspire your associates and enable them to produce their best work.

❑ You move comfortably among a broad range of styles and cultures, and you intuitively personalize your interactions. Consciously and proactively make full use of these talents by leading diversity and community efforts in your organization.

LEADING *OTHERS* WITH STRONG INDIVIDUALIZATION

❑ Ask this person to serve on your selection committee. She will probably be a very good judge of each candidate's strengths and weaknesses. By figuring out the right people for the right roles using her Individualization talents, she will also help improve the organization's productivity.

❑ When appropriate, have this person help design pay-for-performance programs in which all employees can use their strengths to maximize their pay.

❑ Ask this person to teach an internal training class or mentor new employees. She may well have a knack for spotting how each person learns differently.

❑ Look at this person's other dominant themes. If her Developer and Arranger talents are also strong, she may have the potential to be a manager or supervisor. If her talents lie in Command and Woo, she will probably be very effective at turning prospects into customers.

LEADING WITH INPUT

People strong in the Input theme have a craving to know more. Often they like to collect and archive all kinds of information.

BUILD TRUST

- ❏ Become a trusted authority by making sure that the information you provide is both current and accurate. Check multiple sources just to be sure, and help others distinguish between fact and opinion.

- ❏ You earn respect by doing your homework and providing others with the information they need to succeed. When they see that you have put in the time and taken the responsibility to do thorough research, they can't help but appreciate your desire to do good work and trust your comprehensive findings.

SHOW COMPASSION

- ❏ People will be attracted to you as a leader because they see your resourcefulness and your awareness of the most recent developments and information. Let others know that you love to answer their questions and research their most pressing issues. Use your Input talents to connect with others, and make yourself available as someone they can depend on for help.

- ❏ When you meet others who share your interests, think beyond the learning opportunity at hand, and consider the relationship possibilities. Could this be the start of a friendship? Invite this person along when you discover opportunities to pursue your mutual interest, such as an exhibit or an upcoming speech. Use your Input talents as a stepping stone to relationships, and extend the first invitation.

PROVIDE STABILITY

☐ Your knowledge base can be a foundation for stability. When others know that you have researched the topic at hand with your characteristic thoroughness and depth, they will feel confident that your decisions are well thought out. Share with them the extent of your research efforts.

☐ You don't merely collect information, you store it for a time when it might prove useful. By producing the backup and documentation for efforts that might seem risky to some, you assure them that they are moving in the right direction.

CREATE HOPE

☐ Your mind is like a sponge — you naturally soak up information. But just as the primary purpose of a sponge is not to permanently contain what it absorbs, neither should your mind simply store information. Input without output can lead to stagnation. As you gather and absorb information, be aware of the individuals and groups that can benefit from your knowledge, and be intentional about sharing it with them.

☐ Expose yourself to the written thoughts and ideas of other people. Then engage in serious discussion about them. Through this process, you will become a learner who also teaches.

LEADING *OTHERS* WITH STRONG INPUT

☐ Focus this person's natural inquisitiveness by asking him to study a topic that is important to your organization. Or position him in a role with a heavy research component. He enjoys the knowledge that comes from research.

☐ Pay attention to this person's other strong themes. If he is also strong in Developer, he may excel as a teacher or trainer by peppering his lessons with intriguing facts and stories.

❑ Help this person develop a system for storing the information he collects. This system will ensure that he can find it when he and the organization need it.

LEADING WITH INTELLECTION

> People strong in the Intellection theme are characterized by their intellectual activity. They are introspective and appreciate intellectual discussions.

BUILD TRUST

☐ When you carefully analyze others' thinking and then respectfully give your honest opinion, you can help them avoid pitfalls and mistakes. They will appreciate your forthright willingness to help them succeed, and they will come to depend on you for this.

☐ Your sheer intellectual capacity will cause some to respect and revere you. Prove yourself worthy by remembering that thought without action is not always particularly helpful. Use your gift of Intellection to make a difference, and your respect will be well-deserved.

SHOW COMPASSION

☐ Engaging others in intellectual and philosophical debate is one way you make sense of things. It is also one way you build relationships. Channel your provocative questions to people who similarly enjoy the give and take of debate. They will seek you out as a friend and colleague who sharpens their thinking — and one they want to spend time with again and again.

☐ Some people will want you to think with them, while others will want you to think for them. You may be able to build relationships with some people because you look at things from an entirely different angle than they do. For people who are single-minded and action-oriented, you may be the kind of thinking partner who improves their odds for success. Show that you truly care about them by sharing your thoughts with them.

PROVIDE STABILITY

- ❏ Remember to occasionally back up so others can follow the trail of your thinking. They may not be ready for the pronouncement until they have followed the path. Share the mental steps you executed to arrive at your current conclusions so people don't worry that your thinking lacks foundation.

- ❏ Help others understand your need for solitude and space to think. Let them know that this is simply a reflection of your intellectual style and that it results from a desire to bring the most you can to relationships and opportunities. Sharing the fact that you think deeply about what's best for them and for the organization can be a great comfort.

CREATE HOPE

- ❏ Encourage others to use their full intellectual capital by reframing questions for them and by engaging them in dialogue. At the same time, recognize that there will be some who find this intimidating and who need time to reflect before being put on the spot. Help them engage their intellect in the way that is best for them. Then inspire them to use that way of thinking to dream and meditate about the future.

- ❏ Others will seek out your opinion because they appreciate the wise scrutiny you give to ideas and efforts. Bear in mind that you are at your best when you have the time to follow an intellectual trail and see where it leads. Get involved on the front end of projects and initiatives so that your thinking can have a greater impact on long-term outcomes.

LEADING *OTHERS* WITH STRONG INTELLECTION

- ❏ Encourage this person to find long stretches of time when she can simply muse. For some people, pure thinking time is not productive, but for her, it most certainly is. She will emerge from quiet periods of reflection with more clarity and self-confidence.

❑ Have a detailed discussion with this person regarding her strengths. She will probably enjoy the introspection and self-discovery.

❑ Give this person the opportunity to present her views to other people in the department. The pressure of communicating her ideas to others will force her to refine and clarify her thoughts.

❑ Be prepared to team up this person with someone who has strong Activator talents. This partner will push her to act on her thoughts and ideas.

LEADING WITH LEARNER

> People strong in the Learner theme have a great desire to learn
> and want to continuously improve. In particular, the process of
> learning, rather than the outcome, excites them.

BUILD TRUST

❑   Be honest enough to admit that you're still learning. Being
vulnerable and open about your own learning puts you on
par with others and indicates a mutual, not a one-sided,
expectation.

❑   Respect knowledge that is superior to your own. Some
leaders feel the need to be more "advanced" than their
followers in every area. This is unrealistic and unproductive;
it impedes progress. Show your respect through your interest
and appreciation of what others know and are capable of
knowing. Listen to them, and trust them to be experts in
these topics.

SHOW COMPASSION

❑   Co-learning creates mutual vulnerability and discovery.
When you "sign up" for learning, always consider whom you
can invite to learn with you. When you care enough to ask
someone else to join in your learning, you create a shared
memory and a common opportunity that forges a bond.

❑   Appreciate and celebrate others' learning, be it a project
completed, a certification, a good spelling test, or an
improvement on a report card. Let others know that you
understand the hard work and effort that goes into personal
growth. Emphasize that the outcome is exciting, but you
recognize the merit of their journey as well. Affirm that
learning has value, as does the learner.

PROVIDE STABILITY

- ❑ When you invest in another person's growth, you're saying, "You matter. You are here for the long term. You are worth my investment." This helps others know that you expect an enduring — not fleeting — relationship with them. Confirm that sentiment by saying it out loud. Tell people that you're committed to them for the long haul.

- ❑ Learning takes time. Your patience with others as they learn conveys to them that they're not disposable, but rather that you believe in their value and will stand beside them as they develop.

CREATE HOPE

- ❑ Recognize that your enthusiasm for learning may be shared by many in your organization. Ignite this passion by creating an ongoing, organization-wide learning program.

- ❑ Research supports the link between learning and performance. When people have the opportunity to learn and grow, they are more engaged, more productive, and loyal. Look for ways to measure whether people feel their learning needs are being met, to create individualized learning milestones, and to reward achievements in learning. These rewards and seeing measurable progress can inspire others to even greater learning goals.

LEADING *OTHERS* WITH STRONG LEARNER

- ❑ Position this person in roles that require him to stay current in a fast-changing field. He will enjoy the challenge of maintaining his competency.

- ❑ Regardless of this person's role, he will be eager to learn new facts, skills, or knowledge. Explore innovative ways for him to learn and remain motivated, or he may start hunting for a richer learning environment. For example, if he lacks opportunities to learn on the job, encourage him to take courses at the local college. Remember, he doesn't necessarily need to be promoted; he just needs to be learning. It is the process of learning, not necessarily the result, that energizes him.

❑ Encourage this person to become the master or resident expert in his field. Arrange for him to take the relevant classes to accomplish this. If necessary, help him secure financial support to continue his education. Be sure to recognize his learning.

❑ Have this person work beside an expert who will continuously push him to learn more.

❑ Ask this person to conduct internal discussion groups or presentations. There may be no better way to learn than to teach others.

LEADING WITH MAXIMIZER

> People strong in the Maximizer theme focus on strengths as a way to stimulate personal and group excellence. They seek to transform something strong into something superb.

BUILD TRUST

- ❏ Admit that you do some things well and others not so well. Allow people to admit that they too have areas where they consistently struggle. Simply being open can give others permission to be themselves in an honest way.

- ❏ Others will need to hear your message more than once before they believe that you're truly expecting them to shine where they shine and that you're avoiding their "dull spots." Repeat the message so it is heard, understood, and trusted. Some people may need to know that you're not going to surprise them later with an accounting of where they are weak or how they have failed. Continually focus on their excellence until they can truly trust that this will always be your emphasis.

SHOW COMPASSION

- ❏ Use your Maximizer talents to set others free. Too often, people think they have to live up to expectations to be a jack of all trades, a straight-A student, or a well-rounded citizen. Make it clear that you appreciate their unique gifts, their personal brilliance. You don't expect all things from all people — you expect people to be more of who they already are. You may be the only one in people's lives who sees their gifts and talents this way.

- ❏ Sometimes people don't recognize their own areas of brilliance. You can be the one who leads them to the light. Point out moments of excellence you see in others' performance. Tell them that you see the areas where they are truly gifted. We sometimes limit the notion of "talent" to obvious areas like sports or music. Broaden people's view of giftedness. Tell people if they are a gifted friend, a gifted organizer, or a gifted accommodator. Broaden their view of self. You can change a life and become a personal champion.

PROVIDE STABILITY

❑ The surest way to destroy other people's sense of security is to ask them to repeatedly do something for which they are not adequately equipped. Instead, allow others to do and build on what they do best, and watch their confidence grow.

❑ Support others in the areas in which they don't excel. Give them confidence by helping them find complementary partners or systems that free them from failure.

CREATE HOPE

❑ Don't let your Maximizer talents be stifled by conventional wisdom, which says you should find what is broken and fix it. Identify and invest in the aspects of people and organizations that are working. Make sure that most of your resources are spent building up and encouraging these pockets of excellence.

❑ Explain Maximizer concepts to those who may not have ever considered pursuing only what they do well. Point out the advantages of a life lived by these principles: Capitalizing on the gifts with which you've been blessed is more productive. It sets higher expectations, not lower ones. It is the most effective and efficient use of energy and resources. And it's more fun.

❑ You will probably not have the opportunity to observe everything people do exceptionally well. So encourage others to be the keepers and tenders of their own talents. Ask them to study their successes: What did they do best in winning situations? How can they do more of that?

Inspire them to dream. Tell them they can come to you for these kinds of discussions — that this is one of your great pleasures in life. Transfer the ownership of their gifts to them, and support that ownership.

❑ As a leader, you have a responsibility to make the most of your organization's resources — and talent is every company's greatest resource. You see talent in others. Use your authority to help your associates see their own talents and to maximize those talents by positioning people where they can develop and apply strengths. For every need, there is a person with a gift to match. Recruit and select carefully, and you'll have an organization full of opportunities for brilliance.

LEADING *OTHERS* WITH STRONG MAXIMIZER

❑ Schedule time with this person to discuss her strengths in detail and to strategize how and where these strengths can be used to the organization's advantage. She will enjoy these conversations and offer many practical suggestions for how her talents can best be put to use.

❑ As much as possible, help this person develop a career path and a compensation plan that will allow her to keep growing toward excellence in her role. She will instinctively want to stay on a strengths path and may dislike career structures that force her off this path to increase her earning power.

❑ Ask this person to lead a task force to investigate the best practices in your organization. Also ask her to help design a program for measuring and celebrating the productivity of each employee. She will enjoy thinking about what excellence should look like across the organization as well as within each role.

LEADING WITH POSITIVITY

People strong in the Positivity theme have an enthusiasm that is contagious. They are upbeat and can get others excited about what they are going to do.

BUILD TRUST

- ❑ Some people are so accustomed to hearing the negatives pointed out that initially, they will be suspicious of your continued positive remarks. Keep those remarks coming, and allow others to trust, over time, that you're always going to have that upbeat emphasis — in your life and in theirs.

- ❑ Make certain that your praise is always genuine, never empty or false. Research shows that more damage is done through false praise than through criticism. If you believe it, say it. If you don't, show your respect for others' intelligence and discernment, and don't yield to the temptation of false flattery.

SHOW COMPASSION

- ❑ Your Positivity makes you naturally liberal with praise. You can't be too generous — precious few people believe that they are suffering from too much recognition in their lives. Give praise freely. Make it specific. Make it personal. Spread good feelings and genuine appreciation for others. Help others look forward to every interaction they have with you.

- ❑ In hard times, you may be one of the few bright spots in someone's life — a beacon. Never underestimate that role. People will come to you because they need the boost you consistently provide. Let them know that they can. Ask them what they need. You will refresh them.

- ❑ Be the person whose humor is always positive and encouraging. Because of your outlook, you don't resort to deprecating, callous humor or sarcasm. This positive approach will surely rub off on others, and you'll influence the atmosphere around you.

PROVIDE STABILITY

❑ You have a natural talent to increase people's confidence. Look for ways to catch people doing things right or doing the right things. Affirm them. Watch them become stronger and more certain of themselves as a result of your praise.

❑ Your optimism allows you to live with solutions that are sometimes less than perfect. As a result, you encourage others to make progress rather than insisting on perfection. Continue to look for and describe to others the potential that exists in less-than-ideal situations. By doing so, you encourage them to feel free to take risks to improve a situation, even when they don't yet have the total solution.

CREATE HOPE

❑ Play up the drama of moments. If everyone deserves 15 minutes of fame, perhaps you are the person to set the stage. Make each person's 15 minutes big enough to count and important enough to last.

❑ Your optimism helps others look to the future with anticipation. Talk about the future. Talk about what is possible. Ask others to share the opportunities and possibilities they see. Just saying them out loud helps them become expectations, and eventually, realities.

❑ Sometimes feelings are the result of action; other times, feelings are the cause for action. Insist on celebrations, employ the therapy of laughter, and inject music and drama into your organization. This positive impact on the emotional economy will influence your productivity, mutual support, and bottom line.

❑ As you create positive environments, be sure to protect and nurture them. As much as possible, insulate yourself and others from chronic whiners, complainers, and malcontents.

Prune negativity — it's as contagious as your positivity. You and your group must intentionally spend time in highly positive environments that will invigorate and feed optimism.

LEADING *OTHERS* WITH STRONG POSITIVITY

❑ Ask this person to help plan events that your organization hosts for your best customers, such as new product launches or user groups.

❑ This person's enthusiasm is contagious. Consider this when placing him on project teams.

❑ This person likes to celebrate. When milestones of achievement have been reached, ask him for ideas about how to recognize and commemorate the accomplishment. He will be more creative than most.

❑ Pay attention to this person's other top themes. If he also possesses strong Developer talents, he may prove to be an excellent trainer or teacher because he brings excitement to a classroom. If Command is one of his strongest themes, he may excel at selling because he is armed with a potent combination of assertiveness and energy.

LEADING WITH RELATOR

People who are strong in the Relator theme enjoy close relationships with others. They find deep satisfaction in working hard with friends to achieve a goal.

BUILD TRUST

- ❑ Important relationships generate confidences. Maintain and build on the trust you have by keeping the confidences with which you are entrusted. One breach empties a dam.

- ❑ You know that the deepening of a friendship carries inherent risk, but you're more comfortable than most in accepting that fact. Say so. Acknowledge it aloud, and tell the other person that the depth of the relationship has created trust on your part and makes you feel safe with disclosure.

SHOW COMPASSION

- ❑ Make sure you get enough one-on-one time with the key people in your life. Solidify relationships and create emotional energy to share with others. This is what endures. Don't miss opportunities to show that you care.

- ❑ As a strong Relator, you may get and give more love and friendship than most people. Tell others that your relationship with them creates happiness in your life. Ask them how it can enhance their happiness. Show them that you care about the quality of their lives by extending compassion, thoughtfulness, and interest in their well-being.

PROVIDE STABILITY

- ❑ Long-term, close friendships are deeply fulfilling for you. These might be in your family, your personal circle, or your organization. Tell others that you expect these relationships to last your whole life. Set an expectation of ongoing mutual support, understanding, and stability.

❏ You are more at home in situations characterized by informal, rather than formal, systems. But organizations that are growing in size and complexity are likely to require systems that are more formalized. Even in the face of such workplace realities, you can help others know that the core importance of relationships remains constant. Create an informal island in the midst of the vast formal sea of your organization.

CREATE HOPE

❏ You are a giver, not a taker. But for your generosity to continue, you must ensure that the inflow keeps up with the rapid outflow. Identify the people and events that really fulfill you, and schedule time for them. This will give you even more energy to share with those who look to you for hope.

❏ You build relationships that last, giving you a unique depth of perspective on other people's lives and triumphs. Help them see the big view. Point out their achievements and patterns of success. Show them in as many ways as you can that their life has made a difference.

LEADING *OTHERS* WITH STRONG RELATOR

❏ Help this person identify her colleagues' goals. She is more likely to bond with them when she understands their aims and aspirations.

❏ Think about asking this person to build genuine relationships with the critical people you want to retain. She can be a key employee who can help keep good contributors in your organization through relationship building.

❏ Pay attention to this person's other strong themes. If she also shows strong evidence of Focus, Arranger, or Self-Assurance talents, she may have the potential to manage others.

Employees will always work harder for someone they know will be there for them and who wants them to succeed. She can easily establish these kinds of relationships.

❏ This person may very well have the gift of generosity. Draw her attention to it, and show her how her generosity helps her influence and connect with those around her. She will appreciate your noticing, and your own relationship with her will be strengthened.

LEADING WITH RESPONSIBILITY

People strong in the Responsibility theme take psychological ownership of what they say they will do. They are committed to stable values such as honesty and loyalty.

BUILD TRUST

- ❑ You may be the moral conscience for others. When a person or an organization is involved in something that seems wrong, an alarm in your head will go off, and you will feel compelled to address that issue. Go to the source first; ask questions to ascertain the reality and the motive. State your concerns honestly. Whenever possible and ethical, allow the person to correct the situation on his or her own. If necessary, take the next step to right the wrong and assuage your conscience.

- ❑ It's important to appreciate and recognize people of moral strength and integrity. Make sure you acknowledge and affirm what's right at least as often — and preferably more often — than you point out what's wrong. Others will notice and respect you for this.

SHOW COMPASSION

- ❑ You can't help but feel responsible for others, especially for the people you care about most. Check in with them frequently: How are they doing? How can you help? Show your compassion every day, if you can, and know that you are adding warmth to their lives.

- ❑ When you make a mistake that affects someone else, go to that person as quickly as you can and try to make it right. Apologize, certainly, but go beyond apology to restitution. Own your errors in relationships and you will find yourself more easily forgiven. Intimacy will be more quickly restored.

PROVIDE STABILITY

❑ Your sense of responsibility naturally creates a feeling of security in others. They know they can depend on you to make sure things get done properly and on time. Rather than shouldering all of the responsibility yourself, share some of it so that each team member is contributing to the stability of the group.

❑ You're a leader who likes to serve. The service concept is often applied to customers, members, and patrons, but sometimes overlooked when applied to one's followers. Let your followers know about your desire to serve and support them — and that asking for your help is a form of recognition that you appreciate.

CREATE HOPE

❑ You naturally take ownership of every project you're involved in. Share responsibility by encouraging others to do the same. Be their champion, and proactively guide them through the opportunity to experience the challenges of ownership. In doing so, you will contribute to their growth and development.

❑ Psychological ownership is a product of making choices. Rather than assigning responsibilities, invoke ownership by allowing people to choose what they will be responsible for contributing. Let them initiate true responsibility beyond merely accepting assignments.

LEADING *OTHERS* WITH STRONG RESPONSIBILITY

❑ As much as possible, avoid putting this person in team situations with lackadaisical colleagues.

❑ Recognize that this person is a self-starter and requires little supervision to ensure that assignments are completed.

❑ Put this person in positions that require unimpeachable ethics. He will not let you down.

❏ Periodically ask this person what new responsibility he would like to assume. It's motivational for him to volunteer, so give him the opportunity.

❏ This person may well impress you with his ability to deliver time and again, leading you to consider promoting him to management. *Be careful.* He may much prefer to do a job himself than be responsible for someone else's work, in which case he will find managing others frustrating. It might be better to help him find other ways to grow within the organization.

LEADING WITH RESTORATIVE

> People strong in the Restorative theme are adept at dealing with problems. They are good at figuring out what is wrong and resolving it.

BUILD TRUST

- ❏ People trust you because you close the loop, reinstate order, and clean up messes. You restore integrity to systems and make certain that they perform reliably. Let people know that you're willing to do this whenever the need occurs, and they will come to depend on you.

- ❏ You're attracted to situations that others may deem "impossible." Tell others that the more it seems like the odds are against you, the more motivated you are to resolve the problem and make things right. They will respect the intensity of your desire to tackle the tough jobs and learn to rely on you.

SHOW COMPASSION

- ❏ People have such appreciation for your willingness to jump in and solve problems. Your desire to put things right is a sign that you care. Solve problems before others are even aware they exist, and let people know that you did. It will demonstrate your concern and commitment.

- ❏ Perhaps you are most needed when people themselves feel broken. Your instincts are to run to them and offer your emotional support. Be a first responder — reach people in need as quickly as you can, and offer your support and love. They will always remember that you helped them heal from physical or emotional pain, and they will count you among their closest supporters.

PROVIDE STABILITY

☐ You are naturally drawn to turnaround situations. Use your Restorative talents to devise a plan of attack to revitalize a flagging project, organization, business, or team. Others will feel safer knowing you are on the case.

☐ Use your Restorative talents to think of ways to "problem proof" schedules, systems, and efforts. Knowing that you have done the contingency analysis and taken precautions to prevent mistakes helps others feel secure.

CREATE HOPE

☐ Use your Restorative talents to be the one who asks "How do we take it to the next level?" Done is never done because improvement is always possible. Be the instigator and inspiration for ever-higher levels of achievement and service.

☐ Make certain others don't think that all you can see are flaws and shortcomings. Appreciate people for current levels of service and performance. And when they suggest a way to get even better, encourage their desire for excellence.

LEADING *OTHERS* WITH STRONG RESTORATIVE

☐ Position this person in a role in which she is paid to solve problems for your best customers. She enjoys the challenge of discovering and removing obstacles.

☐ When this person resolves a problem, make sure to celebrate the achievement. Every wrong situation righted is a success for her, and she will need you to view it as such. Show her that others have come to rely on her ability to dismantle obstacles and move forward.

☐ Ask this person how she would like to improve. Agree that these improvements should serve as goals for the following six months. She will appreciate this kind of attention and precision.

LEADING WITH SELF-ASSURANCE

People strong in the Self-Assurance theme feel confident in their ability to manage their own lives. They possess an inner compass that gives them confidence that their decisions are right.

BUILD TRUST

❏ Surprise others by admitting the mistakes, wrong turns, and poor decisions you've made in the past. People may not expect someone who is so confident to willingly disclose failures. Actually, conquering your failures is what has made you certain that you can overcome whatever challenges you face. Be vulnerable, and show others that your strength springs from that very vulnerability. It will help them trust that you are genuine.

❏ Share the fact that you sometimes face fears when you make decisions. It's not that you don't find decisions daunting — you simply ask yourself, "If not me, then who?" Once you have the best information you can gather, you know that it's time to take action. By better understanding how you approach decision making, others can see that you are indeed trustworthy.

SHOW COMPASSION

❏ Some people are drawn to you because of your Self-Assurance; your confidence bolsters theirs. They may not give themselves the credit they deserve for their ability to make good decisions, build solid relationships, or create success in their lives. Your belief system says "Of course you can!" You remember their successes much more than their failures, and you can readily recall them in detail. With a cheering, supportive friend like you, they can venture out and try.

❑ You are undeniably independent and self-sufficient — and yet you need to give and receive love. You are human, after all. When you build a relationship, consider what you can contribute to someone else's life. And consider what they can contribute to yours. If you don't need anyone, how can the important people in your life feel valued? Think about how others make your life happier and more fulfilled, and let them know. Tell them you need them. Tell them why.

PROVIDE STABILITY

❑ Confidence — you have it in spades. Share stories of previous successes to help others realize that your confidence is based in experience. That will calm people when you choose a huge goal and say, "We can do it."

❑ "If you must, you can." Use this adage to help people understand that when there are no options, they have the strength and wherewithal to do what is required of them. Inaction is not an option. The only choice is to make the best decision with the available facts, and make a move.

❑ When considering a new task or venture, carefully reflect on the talents, skills, and knowledge it will require. Assemble a solid team, and be prepared to give the helm to someone else if your talents aren't the best fit for the role. People will appreciate your capacity to defer to an expert and make certain they are in capable hands. This will give them comfort and security.

CREATE HOPE

❑ Set ambitious goals. Don't hesitate to reach for what others see as impractical and impossible — but what you see as merely bold and exciting, and most importantly, achievable with some heroics and a little luck. Your Self-Assurance talents can lead you, your family, your colleagues, and your organization to achievements that they would otherwise not have imagined.

❑ Ask others if they have set their goals high enough. They may not dare to dream as big as you do. If you can contribute to a loftier picture than they currently see, you can launch bigger lives.

LEADING *OTHERS* WITH STRONG SELF-ASSURANCE

❑ Position this person in a role where persistence is essential to success. He has the self-confidence to stay the course despite pressure to change direction.

❑ Give this person a role that demands an aura of certainty and stability. At critical moments, his inner authority will calm his colleagues and his customers.

❑ Support this person's self-concept that he is an agent of action. Reinforce it with comments such as "It's up to you. You make it happen," or "What is your intuition saying? Let's go with your gut."

❑ Understand that this person may have beliefs about what he can do that might not relate to his actual talents.

❑ If this person has strong talents in themes such as Futuristic, Focus, Significance, or Arranger, he may well be a potential leader within your organization.

LEADING WITH SIGNIFICANCE

People strong in the Significance theme want to be very important in the eyes of others. They are independent and want to be recognized.

BUILD TRUST

- ❑ Share your desire for achieving big goals. Be very candid about what motivates you, and ask the same of others. This will lead to shared trust.

- ❑ Your impact on the world is almost entirely dependent on the number of people who believe in you as a leader. Always be true to who you are, on and off the stage, and people will see your authenticity.

SHOW COMPASSION

- ❑ Your aspirations will usually be higher than other people's. During the long, steep climb toward the summit, be sure to reward yourself and others by recognizing and celebrating milestones. Reiterate the significance of the goal and the importance of each individual's contribution to it. Tell them what valued partners they are in this venture, and back up those words by giving them a stake in the prize. If your partnership is successful, you may be together for a long time.

- ❑ Applause, appreciation, and affirmation from a valued audience will push you to ever-higher levels of performance. Whose approval you do most value? A parent, a sibling, a teacher, a boss? Your significant other? Have you told them how critical their approval is to your very existence? Let them know how much you care about their opinions. Share with them the moments that mattered. Make sure that they understand the power of their perception and the valuable role they play in your motivation and in your life.

PROVIDE STABILITY

- ❑ Lasting impact matters to you. You want to build something that makes a difference beyond the immediate moment. Share that desire with others. Help them know that your vision is not for immediate glory but for the long haul. They will feel better knowing how deep your commitment goes.

- ❑ Leading crucial teams or significant projects brings out your best. Your greatest motivation may come when the stakes are at their highest. Let others know that when the game is on the line, you want the ball. They will be comforted by your confidence to take big risks and carry the responsibility on your own shoulders.

CREATE HOPE

- ❑ You spend time thinking about the heft of what you will achieve and what it will mean to the present as well as to the future. Help others consider their legacy. Ask them what they are all about. What do they want to be known for? What do they want to leave behind? Give them a vision that looks past the moment and helps them assess the choices they are making every day.

- ❑ Your Significance talents often put you in the spotlight. Use this opportunity to direct positive attention toward others. Your ability to champion others and set them up for success may be the best measure of your Significance.

LEADING *OTHERS* WITH STRONG SIGNIFICANCE

- ❑ Arrange for this person to stand out for the right reasons, or she may try to make it happen herself, perhaps inappropriately.

- ❑ Position this person so that she can associate with credible, productive, professional people. She likes to surround herself with the best.

❏ Encourage this person to praise other top achievers in the group. She enjoys making other people feel successful.

❏ When this person makes claims to excellence — and she will — help her picture the strengths she will have to develop to realize these claims. When coaching her, don't ask her to lower her aspirations; instead, suggest that she keep benchmarks for developing the relevant strengths.

❏ Because this person places such a premium on the perceptions of others, her self-esteem can suffer when people don't give her the recognition she deserves. At these times, draw her attention back to her strengths, and encourage her to set new goals based on them. These goals will help reenergize her.

LEADING WITH STRATEGIC

> People strong in the Strategic theme create alternative ways to proceed. Faced with any given scenario, they can quickly spot the relevant patterns and issues.

BUILD TRUST

- ❑ When making decisions, discuss options candidly and thoroughly with those involved. Help them learn to trust your process of examining all alternatives and then working toward the optimal solution.

- ❑ Be aware of your own biases. Are you weighting possibilities objectively or leaning toward personal desires and comfort levels? Give each option its due. Enlist the help of a good thinking partner to ensure that your decisions are made for the right reasons. Others will respect your integrity and your desire for objectivity.

SHOW COMPASSION

- ❑ Apply your strategic thinking to your relationships. Write down a list of the people who have the most positive influence in your life, and then map out specific things you can do to reinvest even more time and effort in each relationship.

- ❑ What are your goals for family? Close friends? What are their goals? Turn your strategic thinking talents toward these intimate partners in your life. Does someone have a dream but is seeing only obstacles? Does someone feel stuck somewhere with no options? You can help others circumvent a rocky path by pointing out alternate routes. Show that you care by helping them discover the possibilities.

PROVIDE STABILITY

❑ Take time to study the strategies employed by effective leaders you respect or admire. Input equals output; the insights you gather are likely to have a stimulating and resourceful effect on your own strategic thinking. Make others aware that you are not bound by your own thinking and that your options and choices are supported by research. When they see the historical perspective and outside counsel you value, they will appreciate the stable foundation upon which your ideas are built.

❑ While others may consider only the tried-and-true route, you also see the many possibilities that could result from taking a road less traveled. Set aside time specifically for considering "what ifs," and position yourself as a leader in that area. Explain your belief that focusing only on what has gone before may be more limiting than it is enlightening, and help others understand that all options will be carefully weighed. Your open-minded consideration will give others a sense of certainty that you are always on the lookout for the best path to take.

CREATE HOPE

❑ Make sure that you are involved on the front end of new initiatives or enterprises. Your innovative yet methodical approach will be critical to the genesis of a venture because it will keep its creators from developing counterproductive tunnel vision. Broaden their view and increase their chances for success.

❑ Your strategic thinking will be necessary to keep an achievable vision from deteriorating into a mere pipe dream. Lead people and organizations to fully consider all possible paths toward making a vision a reality. Wise forethought can remove obstacles before they appear and inspire others to move forward.

❏ Make yourself known as a resource for consultation with those who are stumped by a particular problem or hindered by an obstacle or barrier. By naturally seeing a way when others are convinced there is no way, you will encourage them and lead them to success.

LEADING *OTHERS* WITH STRONG STRATEGIC

❏ Position this person on the leading edge of your organization. His ability to anticipate problems and their solutions will be invaluable. Ask him to sort through all of the possibilities and find the best way forward for your department. Suggest that he report back on the most effective strategy.

❏ Recognize this person's strong Strategic talents by sending him to a strategic planning or future-oriented seminar. The content will sharpen his ideas.

❏ This person is likely to have a talent for putting his ideas and thoughts into words. To refine his thinking, ask him to present his ideas to his colleagues or to write about them for internal distribution.

LEADING WITH WOO

> People strong in the Woo theme love the challenge of meeting new people and winning them over. They derive satisfaction from breaking the ice and making a connection with another person.

BUILD TRUST

❏ You naturally charm others. Be certain that you do it with integrity so they can trust you when it matters. Otherwise, you may have contacts but not followers.

❏ Others may share a good deal of information with you, even on a first meeting. How can you collect and store that information so that individuals feel like their contributions are valued and, when necessary, protected? Invest in a system for maintaining contact with key people and logging important details of conversations. Make sure to exercise discretion when these details may be sensitive so others will trust you and continue to keep in contact.

SHOW COMPASSION

❏ You win friends and fans wherever you go. It's important to you that some of those contacts develop into long-lasting partnerships. Consider how to make those individuals feel a special connection with you — beyond the quick relationship you build with everyone you meet. How can you take important relationships to the next level? Invest the time and consideration necessary to do so.

❏ Leaders continuously build networks of trust, support, and communication by contacting and relating with a wide range of people. By building a constituency, leaders make an impact across barriers of time, distance, and culture. Create a map of your social network to define how broad you can go while still maintaining a genuine connection.

PROVIDE STABILITY

❏ Share the breadth and depth of your network with others. Knowing that you have contacts everywhere can help people feel sure that you are in on the latest information and confident in the support you can expect when you need it.

❏ Get out and talk to your customers and your competitors, or get involved in the community. Effective leaders don't think their influence stops at the organizational walls, but rather recognize the larger network of affiliation and employ their influence within it. Enjoying a wide base of support helps ensure the continued existence of organizations and opportunities for their expansion.

CREATE HOPE

❏ Your Woo talents give you the ability to quicken the pulse of your organization. Recognize the power of your presence and how you can inspire an exchange of ideas. By simply starting conversations that engage your associates and bringing talented people together, you will help dramatically improve individual and organizational performance.

❏ All of your meeting and greeting is sure to produce information that's valuable to others — information from the customers, superiors, and colleagues of those you are trying to help and guide. Wherever you can, spread the good news and not the gossip. Let others know what they're doing well and how they're being perceived. Share with them the product of your wide-ranging influence, and help them feel affirmed when they succeed at pleasing others.

LEADING *OTHERS* WITH STRONG WOO

❏ Place this person at your organization's initial point of contact with the outside world.

❏ Help this person refine her system for remembering the names of the people she meets. Set a goal for her to learn the names of — and a few personal details about — as many customers as possible. She can help your organization make many connections in the marketplace.

❑ Unless this person also has strong talents in themes such as Empathy and Relator, don't expect her to enjoy a role in which she's asked to build close relationships with your customers. Instead, she may prefer to meet and greet, win over, and move on to the next prospect.

❑ This person's strong Woo talents will win you over and cause you to like her. When considering her for new roles and responsibilities, make sure that you look past your fondness to her genuine strengths. Don't let her Woo dazzle you.

❑ If possible, ask this person to be the builder of goodwill for your organization in your community. Have her represent your organization at community clubs and meetings.

THE RESEARCH

The following three sections are intended to provide a high-level overview of the research behind the book *Strengths Based Leadership*. For more detailed information, please go to strengths.gallup.com. Click on the Publications tab and choose *Strengths Based Leadership*. Then, click on the research link.

A: YOUR STRENGTHS: THE RESEARCH BEHIND STRENGTHSFINDER

This section is adapted from the Clifton StrengthsFinder 2.0 Technical Report: Development and Validation *by Asplund, Lopez, Hodges, and Harter (2007).*

INTRODUCTION

The Clifton StrengthsFinder (CSF) is an online measure of personal talent that identifies areas where an individual's greatest potential for building strengths exists. By identifying one's top themes of talent, the CSF provides a starting point in the identification of specific personal talents, and the related supporting materials help individuals discover how to build upon their talents to develop strengths within their roles. The primary application of the CSF is as an evaluation that initiates a strengths-based development process in work and academic settings. As an omnibus assessment based on strengths psychology, its main application has been in the work domain, but it has been used for understanding individuals in a variety of settings — employees, executive teams, students, families, and personal development.

The CSF is not designed or validated for use in employee selection or mental health screening. Given that CSF feedback is provided to foster intrapersonal development, comparisons across profiles of individuals are discouraged.

STRENGTHS THEORY

When educational psychologist Donald O. Clifton first designed the interviews that subsequently became the basis for the CSF, he began by asking, "What would happen if we studied what is right with people?" Thus emerged a philosophy of using talents as the basis for consistent achievement of excellence (strength). Specifically, the strengths philosophy is the assertion that individuals are able to gain far more when they expend effort to build on their greatest talents than when they spend a comparable amount of effort to remediate their weaknesses (Clifton & Harter, 2003).

Clifton hypothesized that these talents were "naturally recurring patterns of thought, feeling, or behavior that can be productively applied" (Hodges & Clifton, 2004, p. 257). "Strengths" are viewed as the result of maximized talents. Specifically, a strength is mastery created when one's most powerful talents are refined with practice and combined with acquired relevant skills and knowledge. The CSF is designed to measure the raw talents that can serve as the foundation of strengths. Thus the purpose of the instrument is to identify "Signature Themes" of talent that serve as a starting point in the discovery of talents that can be productively applied to achieve success.

DEVELOPMENT OF THE CLIFTON STRENGTHSFINDER

Gallup, widely known for its polls (Gallup, 2004; Newport, 2004) and employee selection research (Harter, Hayes, & Schmidt, 2004; Schmidt & Rader, 1999), developed numerous semi-structured interviews to identify talent that could be enhanced and used to pursue positive outcomes in work and school. In the 1990s, under the leadership of Donald O. Clifton, Gallup developed the CSF as an objective measure of personal talent that could be administered online in less than one hour. More than two million employees and students worldwide had completed this measure as of January 2007.

Clifton, over his 50-year career at the University of Nebraska, Selection Research Incorporated, and Gallup, studied "frames of reference" (Clifton, Hollingsworth, & Hall, 1952), teacher-student rapport (Dodge & Clifton, 1956), management (Clifton, 1970; 1975; 1980), and success across a wide variety of domains in business and education (Buckingham & Clifton, 2000; Clifton & Anderson, 2002; Clifton & Nelson, 1992). He based his research and practice on straightforward notions that stood the test of time and empirical scrutiny.

First, he believed that talents could be operationalized, studied, and capitalized upon in work and academic settings. Talents are manifested in life experiences characterized by yearnings, rapid learning, satisfactions, and timelessness. These trait-like "raw materials" are believed to be the products of normal healthy development and successful experiences over childhood and adolescence. "Strengths" are viewed as extension of talent. More precisely, the strength construct combines talents with associated knowledge and skills and is defined as the ability to consistently provide near-perfect performance in a specific task. (Though labeled the Clifton StrengthsFinder, the instrument actually measures the talents that serve as the foundations for strengths development.)

Second, Clifton considered success to be closely associated with personal talents and strengths in addition to the traditional constructs linked with analytical intelligence. In accordance with those beliefs, he worked to identify hundreds of "themes" (categories) of personal talents that predicted work and academic success, and he constructed empirically based, semi-structured interviews for identifying these themes. When developing the interviews, Clifton and analysts examined the prescribed roles of a person (e.g., student, salesperson, administrator); visited the job site or academic setting; identified outstanding performers in these roles and settings; and determined the long-standing thoughts, feelings, and behaviors associated with situational success. Many of the interviews developed provided useful predictions of positive outcomes (Schmidt & Rader, 1999). These interviews subsequently were administered by Gallup analysts to more than two million individuals for the purposes of personal development and employee selection. In the mid-1990s, when considering the creation of an objective measure of talent, Clifton and colleagues systematically reviewed these interviews and the data they generated to capitalize on the accumulated knowledge and experience of Gallup's talent-based practice.

The prominence of dimensions and items relating to motivation and to values in much of the interview research informed the design of an instrument that can identify those enduring human qualities. An initial pool of more than 5,000 items was constructed on the basis of traditional validity evidence. Given the breadth of talent assessed, the pool of items was considered large and diverse.

A smaller pool was derived subsequent to quantitative review of item functioning and a content review of the representativeness of themes and items within themes (with an eye toward the construct validity of the entire assessment). Specifically, evidence used to evaluate the item pairs was taken from a database of criterion-related validity studies, including over 100 predictive validity studies (Schmidt & Rader, 1999). Factor and reliability analyses were conducted in multiple samples to assess the contribution of items to measurement of themes and the consistency and stability of theme scores — thereby achieving the goal of a balance between maximized theme information and efficiency in instrument length. During development phases, a number of sets of items were pilot tested. The items with the strongest psychometric properties (including item correlation to theme) were retained.

In 1999, a 35-theme version of the CSF was launched. After several months of data were collected, researchers revisited the instrument and, based on analyses of theme uniqueness and redundancy, decided on 180 items and 34 themes. Since 1999, some theme names have changed, but the theme descriptions have not changed substantially.

Today, the CSF is available in 24 languages and is modifiable for individuals with disabilities. It has been taken by more than two million individuals all over the world. It is appropriate for administration to adolescents and adults with a reading level of 10th grade or higher. In 2006, Gallup researchers undertook a comprehensive review of CSF psychometrics, which led to some revisions in the instrument. Confirmatory studies (presented in a subsequent section) validate the 34-theme structure in both adult and student populations. In the course of reviewing more than one million cases in multiple studies, some possible improvements in theme validities and reliabilities were identified. Some of these improvements involved rescoring of existing items, whereas some others required the addition of some new items. These new items were drawn from Gallup's library of talent-related items and from researchers' experience in building structured interviews and providing talent feedback. Finally, there were items that had been included in the 180-item version of the CSF but never used in theme scores.

A thorough review of each of these items showed many to be unnecessary as either distracters or scored items. They were consequently removed. The result of all of these item changes was a slight reduction in the length of the instrument, from 180 items to 177.

Researchers both inside and outside of Gallup contributed a number of the investigations into the CSF's continuing reliability, validity, and applicability to both the general population and college students in particular. Those most recent studies have included:

CONFIRMATORY STUDIES:
- Sireci (University of Massachusetts): n = 10,000
- Lopez (University of Kansas), Hodges (Gallup), Harter (Gallup): n = 601,049
- Asplund (Gallup): n = 110,438
- Asplund: n = 250,000
- Asplund: n = 472,850

RELIABILITY STUDIES:
- Schreiner (Azusa Pacific): n = 438
- Lopez, Harter, Hodges: n = 706
- Asplund: n = 110,438
- Asplund: n = 250,000
- Asplund: n = 472,850

OTHER VALIDITY STUDIES:
- Lopez, Hodges, Harter: n = 297
- Schreiner: n = 438
- Stone (Harvard): n = 278

UTILITY STUDIES:

- Asplund: n = 90,000 employees in more than 900 business units
- Various additional case studies

Separately, each of these studies affirms the ongoing viability of the CSF. More importantly, the collective evidence of all this work is convergent regarding the psychometric properties of the CSF, as well as regarding the details of its validity.

Notwithstanding the confirmatory evidence provided by this body of research, Gallup researchers identified some areas in which the CSF could be improved psychometrically. In particular, it was observed that some of the items could be improved, removed, or replaced. As a logical first step to improving the psychometrics, Gallup researchers thoroughly examined each unscored statement to see whether it could be used to improve the performance of the assessment. Unscored statements that showed no utility were removed, if possible. (Several of the unscored statements are paired with a scored statement, and therefore are not subject for removal at this time.)

ADMINISTRATION AND FEEDBACK

Feedback varies in accordance with the reason the person completes the CSF. Summary scores are not provided to respondents. In most cases, the respondent receives a report listing his or her top five talent themes — those in which the person received his or her highest scores, in order of intensity — the aforementioned "Signature Themes." In other situations, the respondent may review his or her sequence of all 34 themes, along with "action items" for each theme, in a personal feedback session with a Gallup consultant or in a supervised team-building session with colleagues.

In programs designed to promote strengths-based development, feedback is often accompanied by instruction, experiential learning, and mentoring activities designed to help people make the most of their talents (i.e., develop strengths associated with occupational or educational roles). As part of this update to the CSF, a new, more detailed type of feedback is provided: talent descriptions that go beyond the Signature Themes by looking at item-level responses. These "strengths insights" provide a more customized version of the respondent's Signature Themes report featuring a more in-depth dive into the nuances of what makes her unique, using more than 5,000 new personalized strengths insights that Gallup researchers have discovered in recent years. This feedback based on both theme and item-level data provides a richer description of the particular combination of responses provided by the participant.

APPLICATION: STRENGTHS-BASED DEVELOPMENT

The CSF is often used as a starting point for self-discovery in Gallup strengths-based development programs. After a respondent has completed the assessment and talent feedback is provided, a set of developmental suggestions is customized to the individual's Signature Themes and to her role to help her integrate her talents into a more informed view of self. As the identification and integration stages of strengths development unfold, behavioral change is encouraged. Specifically, the strengths-based development process encourages individuals to build strengths by acquiring skills (i.e., basic abilities) and knowledge (i.e., what you know, including facts and making meaning from experiences) that can complement their greatest talents in application to specific tasks.

The CSF's intended purpose is to facilitate personal development and growth. It is intended and used as a springboard for discussion with managers, friends, colleagues, and advisers and as a tool for self-awareness. CSF results are viewed as a preliminary hypothesis to be verified with the respondent. Accordingly, feedback about talents and strengths development often forms the basis of further interventions that help individuals capitalize on their greatest talents and apply them to new challenges. For this application, the psychometric properties of the instrument are more than adequate.

B: YOUR TEAM: GALLUP'S RESEARCH ON WORK TEAM ENGAGEMENT

For more information on engaging teams throughout your organization, we recommend reading the popular management books First, Break All the Rules *and* 12: The Elements of Great Managing, *which are dedicated to this topic. If you would like more detailed or scholarly information on this subject, please contact Gallup or see the following source:*

Harter, J.K., Schmidt, F.L., & Hayes, T.L. (2002). Business-unit-level relationship between employee satisfaction, employee engagement, and business outcomes: A meta-analysis. *Journal of Applied Psychology, 87* (2), 268-279.

After conducting millions of lengthy surveys and comparing the responses to data on productivity, turnover, and many other outcomes, in 1999, our colleagues at Gallup identified 12 core elements that measure the engagement of a local work team. Whether you lead five people or 500 people, engaging your *immediate* team requires spending time on the basics. Even if you are leading hundreds of people, you likely have a smaller team that looks to you for daily management and guidance. For this group, these elements are the 12 best predictors of engagement and subsequent business outcomes. And for the most part, they are within the control of, and most directly influenced by, the manager or leader employees are closest to at work.

As a result, when it comes to your local team, you can expect to have a more engaged group if your team members can strongly agree with these 12 items:

1. *I know what is expected of me at work.*
2. *I have the materials and equipment I need to do my work right.*
3. *At work, I have the opportunity to do what I do best every day.*

4. *In the last seven days, I have received recognition or praise for doing good work.*

5. *My supervisor, or someone at work, seems to care about me as a person.*

6. *There is someone at work who encourages my development.*

7. *At work, my opinions seem to count.*

8. *The mission or purpose of my company makes me feel my job is important.*

9. *My fellow employees are committed to doing quality work.*

10. *I have a best friend at work.*

11. *In the last six months, someone at work has talked to me about my progress.*

12. *This last year, I have had opportunities at work to learn and grow.*

Some of these elements may be beyond your control, but you can dramatically influence your immediate team's engagement if you start with these 12 basics. The key is to measure your team's responses to these 12 items every 6-12 months and track your progress to ensure that you are doing your best to engage your most important constituency.

Recently, we have also been testing several additional items to determine if a leader who is somewhat removed from frontline employees (e.g., a CEO or General Manager) could have a cascading impact on people throughout the organization, even if several levels of hierarchy exist. After testing all of these items, we were able to narrow them down to three that appeared to be the best predictors of key business outcomes:

1. *The leadership of my company always treats me with respect.*

2. *I am confident in my company's financial future.*

3. *The leadership of my company makes me enthusiastic about the future.*

We have now used these items to survey employees in several industries and countries. We have also conducted national polls to test the effectiveness of these organizational leadership items. Including these three more global, cascading items with the core 12 elements allowed us to sort out just how much was within an executive (or indirect) leader's control and how much was not. Based on our earlier research, many of our colleagues speculated that "it was all about the local workgroup" — and they were quick to dismiss the notion that a CEO could have an impact on someone on the front lines of a large company, at least in a way that we could quantify.

Yet we were able to see and measure such an impact, one that went above and beyond the variance that could be explained by workgroup-level engagement. For example, when we studied how likely employees are to recommend their company's products, we found that, overall, just 56% of people surveyed would advocate their own company's products to a friend. When we looked at engaged employees, that number went up to 86%. Then, when we looked at employees who were both engaged and able to strongly agree with these three leadership items, 95% would recommend their company's products.

So engagement alone boosts this measure by 30 percentage points — and then if employees are fully engaged with the company's leadership, that adds another 9 percentage points. We have looked at this in relationship to several other outcomes and see similar results across the board when employees strongly agree with all three of these key leadership items. Much like the core 12 items, getting to near perfect on this organizational leadership metric is likely to take several years. But if 50 — or 500,000 — people look to you for leadership, these are the best starting points for measuring the impact you are having on your constituency.

C: WHY PEOPLE FOLLOW

OVERVIEW

While countless studies have explored the broader topic of leadership, primarily through a qualitative lens, very little work has been done to examine leadership from the follower's perspective. However, this might be the most relevant information to the millions of people who aspire to lead. This study examined data from Gallup Polls of more than 10,000 people that asked followers to describe what leaders contribute to their lives.

METHODS

The initial data were collected from Gallup Polls of 10,004 U.S. adults (over age 18) conducted from 2005-2006 using Gallup's standard Random Digit Dial (RDD) methodology. In sharp contrast to other analyses conducted on leadership, which are primarily based on case studies, interviews, research with one organization, or convenience samples, this methodology allowed us to look at a fairly representative sampling that can be projected to the entire population (with a sampling error of plus or minus one percentage point, given the sample size). Although the polls were conducted with people who were over the age of 18, respondents were not excluded from the survey if they were unemployed. This allowed us to examine leadership that extends beyond an organization's walls — leadership that is taking place in social networks, schools, churches, and families as well. A two-part question was used for this research. (See Figure 1.)

1. What leader has the most positive influence in your daily life?

    Take a few moments to think about this question if you need to. Once you have someone in mind, please list his or her initials.

    (Interviewer records initials)

2. Now, please list three words that best describe what *this person contributes to your life.*

    a. _____

    b. _____

    c. _____

Figure 1. Primary survey question used for analysis.

The first part of the question asked respondents to identify a specific leader, which required them to isolate the person who has the most positive influence on their life. In theory, asking respondents to provide initials for one specific person likely helped them to identify more specific contributions in the second part of this question. The use of the word "positive" was important because we didn't want to study leaders who have a predominantly negative influence. The last three words of the first part of the question — "your daily life" — were critical to examining the type of leadership that makes a tangible and practical difference on a day-to-day basis. This differentiated the question even more from the typical "Whom do you admire most?" or "Who is the best leader you know?" questions that Gallup and others have asked in the past. Questions like these often result in respondents naming major political, religious, and athletic celebrities.

After respondents identified the leader they were thinking about, Gallup interviewers asked them to list three words that "best describe what this person contributes to your life." It is important to note the focus on what the *leader* contributes to the *follower's* life. Again, traditional studies have concentrated on the qualities of the leader herself and would have framed this question around descriptions of the leader's style. In contrast, the question asked in this survey identifies what the leader is actually adding to the follower's life, which is a very different question. Perhaps most importantly, the fact that Gallup's survey asked for just three words per person made it substantially easier to analyze the content from these surveys, particularly when compared to more open-ended questions.

The word responses were compiled into a single Microsoft Excel file for cleaning and coding. First, the Excel spelling tool was used to find and correct spelling errors in the responses. In certain cases, the Merriam-Webster Online Dictionary was also used to fix spelling errors. Second, any duplicate responses given by a respondent were identified and removed from the word response file. Next, cases where respondents provided more than one word per response were identified. If it was clear that the additional words represented separate concepts, then these additional words were separated out and considered additional responses. Finally, any responses that were unintelligible or that could be considered non-responses were identified and coded.

Once the cleaning and coding stage of the word responses was complete, the data were weighted to be more representative of the U.S. population, and the first three responses from each respondent were removed from the file for word frequency analysis. A weighted word-frequency count was conducted on all of the responses. The counts for each response were ranked from highest to lowest frequency to identify a set of the most frequently mentioned words that best describe what everyday leaders contribute to the lives of the respondents.

RESULTS AND FUTURE RESEARCH

The primary results of this research are presented in Part Three of this book. Based on our initial studies of 10,004 people, the following key themes (or basic needs) emerged:

- **Trust** (other words cited by followers included: *honesty, integrity,* and *respect*)

- **Compassion** (other words cited by followers included: *caring, friendship, happiness,* and *love)*
- **Stability** (other words cited by followers included: *security, strength, support,* and *peace)*
- **Hope** (other words cited by followers included: *direction, faith,* and *guidance)*

As we reviewed the research based on the initial question in Figure 1, we found that more than 85% of respondents selected someone they described as a friend, family member, coworker, teacher, or current manager/immediate supervisor. In the vast majority of cases, the leader who had the most impact was someone very close to the person answering the survey.

What's more, people mentioned a leader they had known for a long time. Another question on this survey was: "How long have you known this person?" and the most common response was *10 years.* More than 75% of the people we surveyed named a person they had know for six or more years, and 90% said they had known the person for three or more years.

To determine if followers have similar needs when it comes to higher level organizational and global leaders, we conducted another study in 2008. For this study, we surveyed an additional 1,000 U.S. adults (over age 18) using Gallup's standard Random Digit Dial (RDD) methodology. This time, we modified the question wording and asked respondents specifically about an "organizational leader" and a "global leader." We also removed the word "daily" to ensure that we were asking about a different level of leadership with these new questions. We used the same follow-up language requesting three words that best describe what this person contributes to the respondents' life. (See Figure 2 and Figure 3.)

1. What organizational leader has the most positive influence in your life?

   Take a few moments to think about this question if you need to. Once you have someone in mind, please list his or her initials.

   (Interviewer records initials)

2. Now, please list three words that best describe what *this person contributes to your life.*

   a. _____
   b. _____
   c. _____

Figure 2. Second (organizational) survey question used for analysis.

1. What global leader has the most positive influence in your life?

   Take a few moments to think about this question if you need to. Once you have someone in mind, please list his or her initials.

   (Interviewer records initials)

2. Now, please list three words that best describe what *this person contributes to your life.*

   a. _____
   b. _____
   c. _____

Figure 3. Third (global) survey question used for analysis.

After reviewing the responses to the modified questions, to our surprise, very little had changed. The sequence of words in the Compassion domain did change slightly compared to the initial study (i.e., a smaller percentage of people used the word "caring," and a larger percentage used the word "compassion"). Yet overall, the same categories and words appeared with remarkable consistency.

The next phase of this follower study (which is currently in progress) will examine the core research question in several countries around the globe. At the time of this book's publication, studies of more than 1,000 adults were underway — using Gallup's standard RDD methodology — in the following countries:

- Australia
- Brazil
- Canada
- China
- India
- Japan
- New Zealand
- Singapore
- Thailand

We have conducted a preliminary review of these data from the predominantly English-speaking countries of Australia, Canada, and New Zealand, where translations of the "please list three words" question were not necessary. Based on this initial review, it appears that followers are using a remarkably similar set of words to describe what they expect of leaders in these three countries. However, a more detailed analysis will be conducted once data from several more countries have been collected. We plan to publish these findings on Gallup's website and in future international editions of this book.

REFERENCES

For the references cited here, the page number and a short phrase corresponding to each reference in the text are listed below. Please note that any statistics *not* cited in this section stem from Gallup research and/or studies conducted specifically for publication in this book.

INTRODUCTION

1   *In a recent Gallup Poll:* Gallup Poll, based on telephone interviews with 1,001 national adults, aged 18 and older, conducted January 2-24, 2006. For results based on this sample, one can say with 95% confidence that the margin of error is ±3 percentage points.

2   *In this study:* Gallup Poll, based on 10,004 telephone interviews with national adults, aged 18 and older, conducted 2005-2006. For results based on this sample, one can say with 95% confidence that the margin of error is ±1 percentage point.

Gallup Poll, based on 1,000 telephone interviews with national adults, aged 18 and older, conducted in 2008. For results based on this sample, one can say with 95% confidence that the margin of error is ±3 percentage points.

2   *In the workplace:* Gallup Poll, based on telephone interviews with 1,009 working adults, aged 18 and older, conducted February 2002. For results based on this sample, one can say with 95% confidence that the margin of error is ±3 percentage points.

PART ONE: INVESTING IN YOUR STRENGTHS

10   *"I've never met an effective leader":* Solomon, D. (2007,
      July 1). Questions for Wesley K. Clark: Generally speaking
      [Electronic version]. *The New York Times Magazine.*

13   *To help aspiring leaders:* Asplund, J., Lopez, S.J., Hodges,
      T., & Harter, J. (2007, February). *The Clifton StrengthsFinder
      2.0 technical report: Development and validation.* Omaha,
      NE: The Gallup Organization.

14   *As you can see in the chart below:* Gallup Poll, based on
      telephone interviews with 1,009 working adults, aged 18
      and older, conducted February 2002. For results based
      on this sample, one can say with 95% confidence that the
      margin of error is ±3 percentage points.

15   *This increase in confidence:* Hodges, T.D., & Clifton, D.O.
      (2004). Strengths-based development in practice. In P.A.
      Linley, & S. Joseph (Eds.), *Positive psychology in practice*
      (pp. 256-268). Hoboken, NJ: John Wiley & Sons.

15   *The awareness of one's strengths:* Judge, T.A., & Hurst, C.
      (2008). How the rich (and happy) get richer (and happier):
      Relationship of core self-evaluations to trajectories in
      attaining work success. *Journal of Applied Psychology, 93,*
      849-863.

16   *The results of this study:* DiPrete, T.A., & Eirich,
      G.M. (2006). Cumulative advantage as a mechanism
      for inequality: A review of theoretical and empirical
      developments. *Annual Review of Sociology, 32,* 271–297.

PART TWO: MAXIMIZING YOUR TEAM

22   *Israeli President Shimon Peres:* Gallup Leadership
      Interview with Shimon Peres conducted on February 21,
      1999.

31   *During her senior year at Princeton:* Kopp, W. (2001).
      *One day, all children . . . : The unlikely triumph of teach
      for America and what I learned along the way.* New York:
      PublicAffairs.

34   *A New York Times headline read:* Chira, S. (1990, June
      20). Princeton student's brainstorm: A peace corps to train
      teachers [Electronic version]. *The New York Times.*

35   *In 2008, we followed up with Wendy Kopp:* Gallup
      Leadership Interview with Wendy Kopp conducted on
      January 25, 2008.

36   *In 2005, one in eight Yale graduates:* Lewin, T. (2005,
      October 2). Top graduates line up to teach to the poor
      [Electronic version]. *The New York Times.*

42   *When you sit in a room with Cooper:* Gallup Leadership
      Interview with Simon Cooper conducted on March 31,
      2008.

42   *Born just outside of London:* Crockett, R.O. (2006, May
      29). Keeping Ritz-Carlton at the top of its game [Electronic
      version]. *BusinessWeek.*

43   *As Cooper studied his customers' attachment:* Robison, J. (2006, October 12). How the Ritz-Carlton is reinventing itself. *Gallup Management Journal.* Retrieved August 27, 2008, from http://gmj.gallup.com/content/24871/How-RitzCarlton-Reinventing-Itself.aspx

45   *When it comes to a guest's engagement:* Michelli, J.A. (2008). *The new gold standard: 5 leadership principles for creating a legendary custom experience courtesy of the Ritz-Carlton hotel company.* New York: McGraw-Hill.

45   *When Cooper introduced this concept:* Sinclair, K. (2002). Putting on the 'nouveau Ritz' [Electronic version]. *Hotel Asia Pacific.*

45   *When questioned in a 2002 interview:* Ibid.

49   *Yet when you speak to Mervyn Davies:* Gallup Leadership Interview with Mervyn Davies conducted on March 5, 2008.

51   *Throughout this process:* Berry, M. (2006, February 7). Passion for people [Electronic version]. *Personnel Today.*

53   *By this time, Davies was a regular:* Inventive and dynamic risk-takers who changed the face of Britain [Electronic version]. (2008, January 10). *The Times.*

53   *But as* **The New York Times:** Timmons, H. (2006, October 6). So far, always the predator, not the prey [Electronic version]. *The New York Times.*

53   *. . . and* **The Economist:** Standard Chartered: The decoupled bank [Electronic version]. (2008, February 28). *The Economist.*

60   *But when we spent some time with Best Buy CEO Brad Anderson:* Gallup Leadership Interview with Brad Anderson conducted on February 27, 2008.

76   *As former United Nations Secretary-General Kofi Annan described:* Gallup Leadership Interview with Kofi Annan conducted on July 27, 1999.

PART THREE: UNDERSTANDING WHY PEOPLE FOLLOW

79   *As legendary investor Warren Buffett put it:* Boden, A., & Ashurov, A. (2003, April 28). A walk in the rain with Warren Buffett [Electronic version]. *The Harbus.*

81   *As Peter Drucker said:* Ward, A. (2006). Looking for leaders [Electronic version]. *Leadership.*

83   *One of our national polls:* Gallup Poll, based on telephone interviews with 1,009 working adults, aged 18 and older, conducted February 2002. For results based on this sample, one can say with 95% confidence that the margin of error is ±3 percentage points.

85   *And we found that people who agree with this statement:* Buckingham, M., & Coffman, C. (1999). *First, break all the rules: What the world's greatest managers do differently.* New York: Simon & Schuster.

87   ***Employees who have high confidence:*** Gallup Polls, based on telephone interviews with 3,008 working adults, aged 18 and older, conducted between April 2004 and May 2005. For results based on this sample, one can say with 95% confidence that the margin of error is ±3 percentage points.

89   ***Sixty-nine percent of employees:*** Gallup Polls, based on telephone interviews with 3,008 working adults, aged 18 and older, conducted between April 2004 and May 2005. For results based on this sample, one can say with 95% confidence that the margin of error is ±3 percentage points.

CONCLUSION: LEADERSHIP THAT LASTS *BEYOND* A LIFETIME

94   ***Martin Luther King Jr. preached:*** Branch, T. (2006, January 1). "I have seen the promised land" [Electronic version]. *Time.*

ADDITIONAL RESOURCES: THE RESEARCH

A: Your Strengths: The Research Behind StrengthsFinder

239   ***Specifically, the strengths philosophy:*** Clifton, D.O., & Harter, J.K. (2003). Strengths investment. In K.S. Cameron, J.E. Dutton, & R.E. Quinn (Eds.), *Positive organizational scholarship.* (pp. 111-121). San Francisco: Berrett-Koehler.

240   ***Clifton hypothesized:*** Hodges, T.D., & Clifton, D.O. (2004). Strengths-based development in practice. In A. Linley & S. Joseph (Eds.), *Handbook of positive psychology in practice.* Hoboken, New Jersey: John Wiley and Sons, Inc.

240   ***Gallup, widely known for its polls:*** Gallup, G. (2004). *The Gallup Poll: Public opinion 2003.* Lanham, MD. Roman and Littlefield.

Newport, F. (2004). *Polling matters.* New York: Warner Books.

240   **. . . *and employee selection research:*** Harter, J.K., Hayes, T.L., & Schmidt, F.L. (2004). *Meta-analytic predictive validity of Gallup Selection Research Instruments* [technical report]. Omaha, NE: The Gallup Organization.

Schmidt, F.L., & Rader, M. (1999). Exploring the boundary conditions for interview validity: Meta-analytic validity findings for a new interview type. *Personnel Psychology, 52,* 445-464.

240   ***Clifton, over his 50-year career:*** Clifton, D.O., Hollingsworth, F.L., & Hall, W.E. (1952). A projective technique for measuring positive and negative attitudes towards people in a real-life situation. *Journal of Educational Psychology, 43.*

240   **. . . *teacher-student rapport:*** Dodge, G.W., & Clifton, D.O. (1956). Teacher-pupil rapport and student teacher characteristics, *Journal of Educational Psychology, 47,* 6.

240   . . . *management:* Clifton, D.O. (1970, March). *The magnificence of management.* A reprint of an address presented to the 8th Annual Life Agency Management Program. Boston, Mass.

Clifton, D.O. (1975). Interaction is: Where the action is. A reprint of a report prepared by Donald O. Clifton and presented at the 1972 Chartered Life Underwriters (CLU) Forum.

Clifton, D.O. (1980). *Varsity Management: A way to increase productivity.* A reprint of an address presented to the 29th Annual Consumer Credit Insurance Association (CCIA) Program on June 24, 1980. Napa, California.

240   . . . *business and education:* Buckingham, M., & Clifton, D.O. (2000). *Now, discover your strengths.* New York: Free Press.

Clifton, D.O., & Anderson, E. (2002). *StrengthsQuest: Discover and develop your strengths in academics, career, and beyond.* New York: Gallup Press.

Clifton, D.O, & Nelson, P. (1992). *Soar with your strengths.* New York: Delacorte Press.

241   *Many of the interviews:* Schmidt, F.L., & Rader, M. (1999). Exploring the boundary conditions for interview validity: Meta-analytic validity findings for a new interview type. *Personnel Psychology, 52,* 445-464.

242   *Specifically, evidence used:* Ibid.

ABOUT THE AUTHOR

TOM RATH

Gallup Global Practice Leader Tom Rath has written two #1 international bestsellers. His first book, *How Full Is Your Bucket?*, was a #1 *New York Times* bestseller, and his most recent book, *StrengthsFinder 2.0*, is a long-running #1 *Wall Street Journal* and #1 *BusinessWeek* bestseller. In total, Rath's books have sold more than a million copies and have made more than 100 appearances on the *Wall Street Journal* bestseller list.

Rath has been with Gallup for 14 years and currently leads Gallup's workplace research and leadership consulting worldwide. He also serves on the board of VHL.org, an organization dedicated to cancer research and patient support.

Rath earned degrees from the University of Michigan and the University of Pennsylvania. He and his wife, Ashley, live in Washington, D.C.

Gallup Press exists to educate and inform the people who govern, manage, teach and lead the world's 7 billion citizens. Each book meets Gallup's requirements of integrity, trust and independence and is based on Gallup-approved science and research.